ANNA MARANTI
ARCHEOLOGIST

OLYMPIA
THE GAMES IN ANTIQUITY

EDITIONS
TOUBI'S

COPYRIGHT   MICHAEL TOUBIS PUBLICATIONS S.A.
                 Nisiza Karela, Koropi, Attica, Greece.
                 Telephone: +30 210 6029974
                 Fax: +30 210 6646856
                 Web Site:http://www.toubis.gr

ISBN: 960-540-336-6

CONTENTS

There are places that speak of the gods, where the gods speak to men. When the world was still young, still full of gods, places like this, so full of meaning, were chosen by the ancient Greeks in order to communicate with their deities. The gentle wooded countryside along the banks of the Alpheios has nothing in common with the bare mountains and intricate, indented coasts of the Greek islands. Similarly, the history of the place is gentle and lacking in the dramatic tension characteristic of the rest of Greece, and it seems to have recommended itself from the very beginning as a meeting place, where Greeks from every corner of Greece and the Mediterranean could gather and engage in peaceful competition around the altar of Olympic Zeus. The altar that had been brought from the north by the Eleians at the dawn of history, and which Herakles erected in the wooded Altis - the sacred grove; Herakles, who gave to the funeral games held in honour of the hero Pelops the name Olympic games. There are words that live on throughout the centuries, independently of the place and circumstances that gave rise to them, gradually losing their meaning and at the same time impoverishing our lives. The adjective "Olympic", which was associated in ancient times with

*one of its most important social events, is nowadays
often used in a very banal sense, a word deprived
of any meaning, a common word, an adjective devoid
of all content, identified on a daily basis with false
language and vulgar exploitation and the debasement
of concepts and values - steps that distance us, rather
than bring us closer to the real meaning of life.*

*To visit Olympia is to return to the true world, the
marvellous world where the beauty of the human body
was cultivated through physical endeavour, and the
spirit of competition and the idea of peace were
developed through noble rivalry. Re-immersion in the
values that constitute the deeper meaning of and
positive assent to life, a re-immersion that is so
necessary today, can be experienced only by those
visitors who come prepared to profit by their experience
of the natural environment and monuments of the
Altis. For over and above its aesthetic value, it is to
those who have acquired knowledge of its history and
religious life that the sanctuary speaks of its wonderful
past, that unique moment in the history of mankind that
gave birth to it and finds expression through it.*
And this is the aim of this little book.

G. Steinhauer

Chapter

1

MYTHS OF OLYMPIA

- HERACLES IDAEUS
- HERACLES
- PELOPS AND HIPPODAMIA
- ZEUS
- ALPHEUS AND ARETHUSA

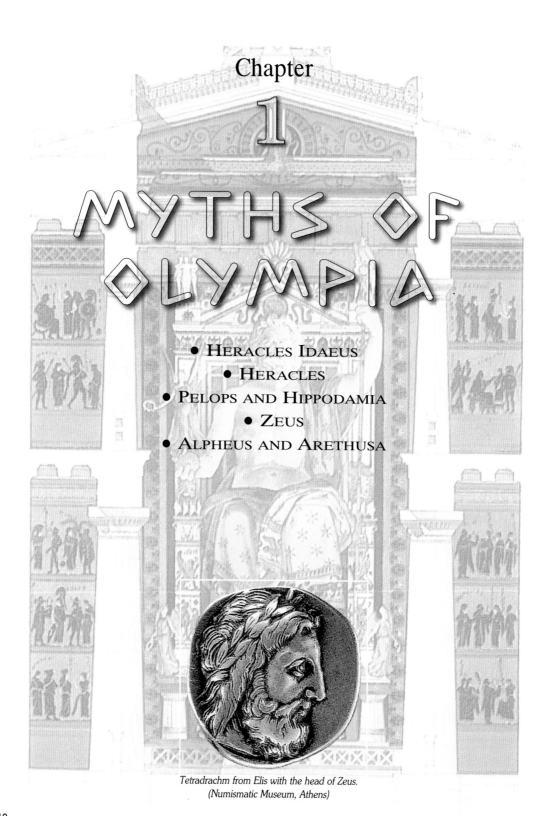

Tetradrachm from Elis with the head of Zeus.
(Numismatic Museum, Athens)

In antiquity, when the fame of a sanctuary spread beyond its immediate borders, it was believed that not only the sanctuary, but also its athletic competitions, were founded by gods and heroes and that they were the first to have taken part in the competitions. The beginnings of the Olympic games are lost, deep in the mists of time, but the myths concerning their foundation are many and varied and reflect the religious beliefs of the different peoples who inhabited the area. One myth names the founder of the games as Heracles Idaeus, who came from Crete with his brothers, the Curetes, and organized a race with a wild olive branch as the prize. Another dominant tradition was that the competitions were organized by Pelops, son of Tantalus, after having beaten Oenomaus in a chariot race. According to other myths, the competitions were established by Zeus after he had beaten Cronus at wrestling, or by Apollo after he had beaten Hermes in a race and Ares in a boxing match. There is also a legend which says that the founder of the competitions was Clymenus of Crete, a descendant of Heracles Idaeus, and another declaring that the competitions were established by Heracles, the famous son of Alcmene. Diodorus informs us that after the end of the Argonautic expedition, Heracles suggested to the leaders and heroes who were preparing to return home that they should vow that if any of them needed help in the future, the others would come to their assistance, and that they should choose a prominent place somewhere in Greece and establish there competitions in honour of Zeus Olympius. The leaders delegated Heracles who chose the site of Olympia which was devoted to Zeus. He established horse races and gymnastic competitions, defined the prizes and the rules of the competitions and sent *Theoroi* (official representatives of the competition committee) to announce them in the towns.

The peaceful landscape of Olympia hosted the wor-

Small bronze group of the Geometric Period from Olympia. Possibly a representation of the battle between Heracles and the Centaur, Nessus. (Metropolitan Museum, New York)

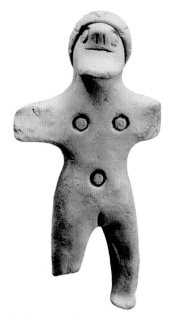

Small terracotta female figurine, possibly Hera, from the second half of the 8th century BC. (Museum of Olympia)

ship of many deities who followed, one after the other, embracing various mythological traditions which are now long forgotten in the depths of time. The data from excavations and mythological study show that the first inhabitants of this area made offerings to a female deity, Gaia, the wife of Uranus. Her sanctuary, the Gaion, was located at the southern foot of the Hill of Cronus which, as the name indicates, was devoted to Cronus, a god of Cretan origin. At the same time, besides Gaia, other gods were also prominently worshipped in the area: Cronus, Rhea, Themis and Heracles Idaeus, the sanctuaries of whom may have been gathered at the foot of the Hill of Cronus. One more important god or demon of the Eleans was Sosipolis, who had a temple in Olympia where he was honoured together with Eilithyia. He was a snake-like divinity who seems to have been very respected, as the Eleans were accustomed to invoking him as the guardian of oaths.

HERACLES IDAEUS

One of the myths related to the birth of the 'Olympia' mentions the Cretan brothers, the Dactyls of Mount Ida or the Curetes. To them Rhea had entrusted the guarding of the newborn Zeus in the Cretan cave of Mount Ida, hence: Zeus Idaeus. From Ida, the five brothers: Heracles, Paeonius, Epimedes, Iasus and Idas (or Acesidas), came to Olympia. The eldest brother, Heracles Idaeus, had his brothers take part in a race and afterwards crowned the winner with a wild olive branch. According to this legend, the Olympic games were founded in the years soon after the time of Cronus, which means a long time before Heracles, the famous son of Amphitryon and Alcmene, was born. Furthermore, Pausanias mentions that Heracles Idaeus named these competitions 'Olympia' and that he decided that they should take place every five years because he and his brothers were five in number. There is evidence of his worship in the area of the Altis at Olympia before the dominance of the worship of Zeus. There was an altar to Heracles and his four brothers, known as the Parastates which, it is said, was built by Clymenus, a descendant of Heracles Idaeus, who had come to Olympia from Crete.

HERACLES

During the time when Elis was ruled by king Augeas, a descendant of Oenomaus, Heracles was sent by Eurystheus to clean the filth from the stables of Augeas, which had built up and was spreading disease through the country. Heracles asked Augeas for one tenth of his flock claiming that he would clean the area in one day. The latter, certain that Heracles would not be able to do this, accepted the agreement. When Heracles successfully completed his task, however, Augeas did not keep his promise and refused to give him the agreed payment. Heracles then started a campaign against him, conquered Elis and killed Augeas. After calling Phyleus from Dulichium, Heracles gave him the kingdom and built altars in Olympia for the gods of Olympus, establishing the Olympic games around them.

Representation of Heracles on a pot from the beginning of the 5th century BC. He has a lion skin and a sword and is holding a club and the tripod he has just taken from the sanctuary at Delphi. (Martin von Wagner Museum, Würtsburg)

Heracles cleaning the Augean stables with the assistance of the goddess Athena. Metope of the 5th century BC from the Temple of Zeus at Olympia. (Archaeological Museum of Olympia)

PELOPS AND HIPPODAMIA

Silver decadrachm from
the beginning of the 4th century BC.

Opposite: The kidnapping of Hippodamia
by Pelops. Red-figure representation
on a krater of the 5th century BC. (Archaeological Museum, Arezzo)

Finely sculptured work of the 5th century BC
from the east pediment of the temple of Zeus,
possibly a representation of Pelops, naked.
It also held a spear and possibly a shield.
(Archaeological Museum of Olympia)

The first evidence relevant to the worship of Pelops and Hippodamia, in the area of Olympia, appeared during the Mycenaean period. The mythological tradition of the area is connected to the ancient king of Pisa, Oenomaus, son of the god Ares. Oenomaus had received a prophecy that the end of his life would come with the marriage of his daughter Hippodamia, whom he begot with his wife Sterope. In an attempt to avoid the prophecy, the king announced that he would give his daughter to the one who would beat him in a chariot race. He, however, used unbeatable weapons and immortal horses, gifts from his father. During the races, many brave young men were killed. Oenomaus buried their bodies close to the Hippodrome of Olympia and nailed their heads over the gates of his palace. The last suitor was Pelops, son of Tantalus, who fell instantly in love with Hippodamia and she with him. The only person who could help them was Oenomaus' charioteer, Myrtilus, son of Hermes and gifted with his father's cunning. Pelops promised to give Myrtilus half of Oenomaus' kingdom if he would help him win. Myrtilus accepted and, before the start of the race, he replaced the axle-pins of the king's chariot with wax pegs which, once the race had started, melted and the wheels fell off. Oenomaus became tangled up in the reins and was killed. Pelops, therefore, won the race and took Hippodamia for his wife along with the whole kingdom of Oenomaus. When Myrtilus later tried to rape Hippodamia, Pelops killed him and then went to Oceanus where he was purified by Hephaestus and returned to become king of Pisa, wise and strong. He also renamed the land, which was formerly called Apia, to Peloponissos (the Island of Pelops), or the Peloponnese.

Without doubt, Pelops was the most important mythical person of the Peloponnese. In the sacred grove of Olympia, the inhabitants founded a sanctuary to honour him at which they would offer sacrifices every year. The belief that the Olympic games were established and took place in memory of Pelops was also very popular.

ZEUS

The sacred site of Olympia had also, from very early on, accepted the worship of Zeus which was brought here, around 2000 BC, by the Greeks coming down from the Balkan peninsula who then settled here permanently. In Homer's 'Iliad', Zeus is the father of gods and men. His weapon is the lightning bolt which makes him invincible and his superiority over both mortals and gods is unquestionable. In the 'Theogeny', Hesiod informs us of the myths concerning the first years of the life of Zeus. Cronus, son of Uranus and Gaia, dethroned his father and took his kingdom. The new king, however, was unable

Fifth century BC bronze statuette of Zeus, holding a lightning bolt, from Dodona. (National Archaeological Museum of Athens)

to rest as he had heard from his parents that, even if he was stronger, one of his male children would overthrow him. Every time Rhea bore him a child, therefore, he swallowed it in the fear that it might depose him. Rhea had no other choice than to trick her husband in order to save her last child, Zeus, and after consulting Uranus and Gaia, she put their risky plan into practice. She wrapped a stone up to give it the appearance of the newborn Zeus and gave it to Cronus who swallowed it instead of their child. Afterwards, Rhea entrusted the infant to the Curetes and the Nymphs, Adrastea and Ida, who raised him on Crete. When Zeus became a man, with the help of Metis he forced Cronus to spit out his brothers Hades and Poseidon. With their help, Zeus then overthrew his father and took his throne. Following this, he fought for nine years against the older gods, the Titans, who did not recognize him as their leader. Zeus beat them, strengthened his own power and became master of the heavens as well as creator and governor of order in the world.

ALPHEUS AND ARETHUSA

There also survives, in Olympia, the myth of Alpheus and Arethusa. Arethusa, a Nymph of Achaea, had returned from Stymphalia where she had been hunting. As she was tired she decided to refresh herself in the waters of Alpheus. When Alpheus saw her naked he was stunned by her beauty and fell passionately in love with her. When he confessed his feelings to her, however, Arethusa ran away wanting to avoid his advances. Alpheus chased her and when they arrived, running, in Elis, the exhausted Arethusa called on Artemis to save her. The goddess then wrapped her in a cloud and brought her to the island of Ortygia close to Syracuse, where she transformed her into a spring. Alpheus did not hesitate to cross the sea to reach Arethusa. He burst into the sea and tried not to mix his waters with the salty waters of the sea on his way so that he could unite with the clean waters of Arethusa.

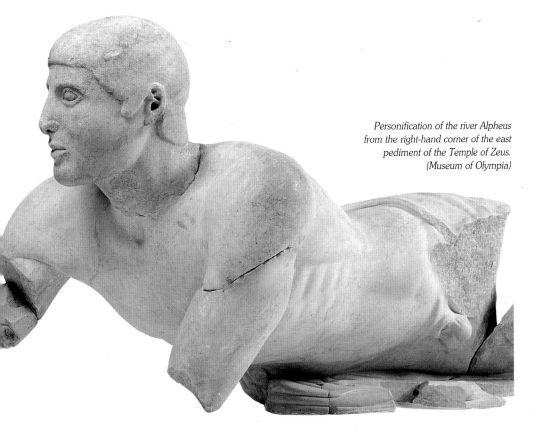

Personification of the river Alpheus from the right-hand corner of the east pediment of the Temple of Zeus. (Museum of Olympia)

17

Chapter
2
HISTORY
OF THE
SANCTUARY

Bronze head of a bull.

In antiquity, Olympia belonged to Pisa, the mythical port in the land of the Epeians. The first king of Pisa was Oenomaus, a contemporary of king Epeius who gave his name to the inhabitants of the surrounding area. His descendants were Aetolus, Heleios, Augeas and many other Homeric heroes such as Amphimachos and Agasthenes.

The first signs of human habitation discovered at Olympia date back to the 3rd millennium BC. These remains were found at the southern foot of the Hill of Cronus and on the Hill of Oenomaus as well as in the area of the New Museum. The finds consist of apsidal houses (with one end rounded), built with irregular stones, along with many handmade tools and pots. There are also finds from the late Helladic period as well as a series of chambered tombs from the Mycenaean period. In these times, worship was dominated by female divinities, the oldest of which was Gaia who is associated with the pre-Hellenic figure of the chthonic Aegean mother-goddess. In addition to Gaia, other deities worshipped at Olympia were Themis, Eilithyia and Cronus. During the Mycenaean period, the worship of the goddess of fertility was connected to the figures of Hera, Demeter and Hippodamia whilst, correspondingly, the god of the mysteries of fertility was identified with Zeus, Heracles Idaeus and Pelops. During the Geometric period (11th - 8th centuries BC), the northwest Peloponnese was settled by the Dorians who came down from the north under their leader Oxylus, king of Elis. These years saw the beginning of the first dispute, between the Pisatans and the new inhabitants of Elis, over the administration of the sanctuary of Olympia and the management of the Olympic games. The start of the Olympic games is buried deep in the age of myth and it is difficult to say when the games actually began. In the historical years, however, the games were reinstated by Iphitus, king of Elis and descendant of Oxylus. A large number of

Bronze group of the Geometric Period showing figurines of seven naked women dancing in a circle.

bronze and terracotta figurines from this period reflect the prosperity of the sanctuary of Olympia but also the gradual dominance of the worship of Zeus.

The 8th century BC was the most important for the further promotion of the sanctuary of Olympia on a nationwide level, as well as for the general establishment of the institution of the Olympic games. By then, the games had acquired a special importance and a panhellenic prestige. Conventionally, the first Olympiad is placed in the year 776 BC when the official recording of the winners began. At this time, Coroebus of Elis won the only game which existed; the stadion, a footrace of one stade (178 - 179 m). From the Olympic winners of the 8th century BC, it can be seen that the fame of the games had spread throughout the whole of the Peloponnese. Iphitus of Elis, together with Lycurgus of Sparta and Cleisthenes of Pisa, agreed that the games should be held every fifth year and established the 'Sacred Truce', an agreement which saw the suspension of hostilities among the states taking part in the games for their duration. The text of this treaty, which was believed to be necessary for the development of the games, was immortalized in writing around the famous bronze disc of Iphitus, which was kept in the temple of Hera up to the time when Pausanias saw it (around AD 160).

THE ARCHAIC PERIOD

During the Archaic period, the indication of the desire of the athletes from all over Greece to take part in the games came parallel with a large number of offerings from the towns and colonies of the Greek world: From southern Italy and Sicily, from eastern and western Greece and also from north Africa. Responsibility for the organization of the Olympic games belonged to the people of Elis despite the vigorous attempts of the Pisatans to take control from them.

More specifically, a short while after the 26th Olympiad (676 BC), the Pisatans occupied Olympia. Some years later, the Eleans, after defeating the Pisatans, gained back the running of the games. The state of Pisa, though somewhat limited, continued however and in the latter half of the 7th century BC it returned led by king Pantaleon, son of Omphalion. Under his

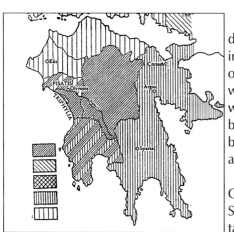

Map showing the distribution of tribes in the Peloponnese: Arcadians, Aeolians, Ionians, Dorians and North West Greeks.

leadership, and with the assistance of the neighbouring nations, the Pisatans occupied Olympia and organized the games of 644 BC. Later, the Eleans again took back Olympia but the Pisatans continued to be a threat. A period of repeated attacks from both sides followed, the last coming from the Pisatans under Pyrros, with the participation of many *perioikoi*, or free men. This attack failed and the victorious Eleans destroyed the Pisatans and their allies. In the middle of the 6th century BC, the Eleans entered into a treaty of 100 years of peace with the inhabitants of the Arcadian town of Eraea. The text of this treaty still survives, carved into a bronze plaque from the sanctuary of Olympia where it hung.

Despite these events, the Archaic period was a time of great prosperity for Olympia which saw countless offerings from the various winners of the events as well as other individuals. Offerings to Zeus Areus consisted mainly of helmets, greaves, shields, cuirasses, swords and spear heads. Economically, the Archaic period was represented by the temple of Hera, the bouleuterion (or council house), a part of the prytaneion (or magistrate's residence) and the treasuries. At the end of the Archaic period, Greece was in some way a nation of athletes. It is E. N. Gardiner's observation that, "the victory of the Greeks over the Persians... was the victory of a handful of trained athletes over the hordes of flabby barbarians".

Colonization

The 8th century BC was a very important period in the history of the ancient Greek world. The colonization which began during the first half of that century, brought Hellenism to all of the Mediterranean region on the coasts of the three continents, from the Iberian peninsula to Libya and up to Crimea. Especially in Sicily and South Italy, Asia Minor and the Black Sea where dense Greek communities gathered. Many of these colonies became large and powerful and had well developed cultures and commercial sea trading.

The areas of settlement of the second Greek colonization.

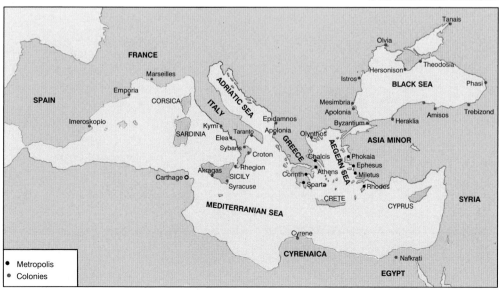

Metropolis
Colonies

THE CLASSICAL PERIOD

During the Classical period that followed, the rise of the sacred site of Olympia was remarkable. In its peaceful location, under the cover of the Sacred Truce, the most important opportunities for the development of a strong feeling of national unity among the Greeks arose and it was, unquestionably, the ideal place in which to apply the principles of a panhellenic politics which called for all Greeks to forget those who separated them and to fight, unified, against their mutual enemies. During the first Olympiad after the Persian wars, in 476 BC, the victor, Themistocles of Salamis, was uniquely honoured by the assembled crowd during his entry to the stadium. After the battle of Plataea, the names of 27 towns who fought against the Persians were engraved on the base of the statue of Zeus which the Greeks offered at Olympia after their victory. Also on public display in the area of the sacred Altis was the 30-year treaty between Athens and Sparta made in 445 BC, as well as the 100-year treaty between Athens, Argos, Elis and Mantinea against Sparta made in 420 BC. The richness of the votive offerings indicates the significance of the panhellenic reputation of the sanctuary.

Decadrachm from the Syracusians known as Demareteion. Circulated immediately after the battle of Himera and the large victory of the Greeks in Sicily over the Carthaginians in 480 BC. (Archaeological Museum of Berlin)

Representation on a red-figured pot showing an ambush with three almost naked kneeling warriors wearing greaves and holding shields and spears.

The Peloponnesian War (431 - 404 BC) undermined the Greek towns and caused many disturbances in the area of Olympia. In 420 BC, the Eleans imposed a penalty of 2000 minae and exclusion from the games upon the Spartans because they had violated the Sacred Truce by invading Lepreus after the Olympic truce had already been declared. All attempts to find a compromise failed and there was a serious risk of the Spartans invading Olympia during the games. The situation became even more threatening when the winner of the two-horse chariot race, Lichas of Lacedaemonia, was thrashed by the rabdouchoi, or rod-bearers, who refused to recognize his victory because his homeland had been excluded from the games. After this, special measures for the security of the sanctuary were taken: the Eleans placed armed young men as guards and 1,000 Argives along with 1,000 Mantineans and Athenian horsemen arrived as reinforcements. The Spartans did not eventually attack and the danger subsided. This, as well as the fact that the Eleans later prevented Agis, king of Sparta, from offering a sacrifice at Olympia, infuriated the Spartans who demanded that the Eleans free their perioikoi and contribute to the war effort against the Athenians. The Eleans, however, turned down these demands and the Spartans sent a military force against them,

Breast plates and shields of bronze. (Museum of Olympia)

led by king Agis, which invaded Elis from the north (in order not to destroy the area of Olympia) a short while before the beginning of the Olympic games of 400 BC. When the Spartan army passed the river Larissus, however, there was a large earthquake which Agis took to be a bad omen from the gods and decided to stop the campaign against the Eleans.

All these events caused much bloodshed between the democrats and oligarchs in Elis, which finally came under Spartan rule in 398 BC when the democratic regime was replaced by an oligarchic one. After many attempts at independence from Sparta, the Eleans eventually fought alongside them after 370 BC. Their aim now was to regain, with the help of their new Spartan allies, all those towns which had once been under their control. The crucial point of the dispute in the year 364 BC was Olympia which, at the time, belonged to the Arcadians. When the 104th Olympiad (of 364 BC) was close to starting, the Arcadians and their dependents the Pisatans, prepared themselves to receive the management of the games, a fact which would make all too clear their domination in the sanctuary of Olympia. The Pisatans, as has been mentioned before, claimed they had founded the games during the Archaic period and that they had organized them at least twice.

The Eleans, on their side, decided to regain the sacred site before the opening of the Olympiad. With the help of the Achaeans they headed towards Olympia, though there was some delay which allowed the Arcadians and the Pisatans to hold the horse race and the races of the pentathlon without any disturbance. When the time came for the wrestling event of the pentathlon, however, the athletes could not compete because the Eleans had meanwhile passed the limits of the precinct. The

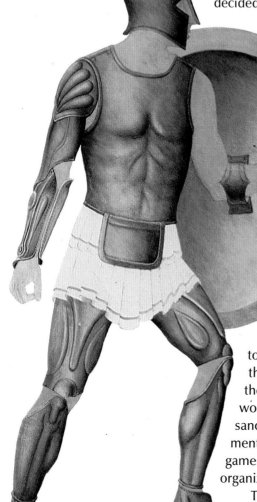

Representation of a Greek warrior in the full defensive armour of antiquity.

Arcadians then lined up along the Cladeus river with the allied forces of the Argives and Athenians. The Eleans attacked and put the Arcadians to flight.

Gaining ground constantly, they reached the area between the sanctuary of Hestia and the bouleuterion, and began to drive the enemy back towards the altar. The spectators of the games stayed in their places, surrounded but calm, and watched the battle going on in front of their eyes, applauding both sides according- ly. The Eleans were exhausted, however, and because of the heavy losses they had sustained, were forced to retreat. The Arcadians and their allies, on the other hand, being afraid that the Eleans would try a new attack the next day, spent all night putting up roughly made field defences to confront them. The next day, upon seeing that these defences were formidable, the Eleans returned home.

Silver tetradrachm circulated after Philip II's victory in the horse race in 356 BC. (Numismatic Museum, Athens)

Important political men like Philip II and Alcibiades of Athens wanted to increase their political prestige by making official appearances· at the Olympic games.

Philip took part in the games himself in 356 BC and won. After the battle of Chaeronea in 338 BC and the victory of the Macedonians, he built the Philippeion at Olympia, both as thanks to Zeus and to underline and emphasize Macedonian power. In 324 BC, Alexander the Great chose the site of Olympia as the place where the Exiles' Decree was acknowledged, which gave general amnesty to all exiles. This decree was delivered by Nicanor and was wildly applauded by the assembled crowd among whom there were 20,000 exiles.

Syracusian silver coin depicting Nike crowning the winner of a four-horse chariot race.

The construction activity of the Classical period produced important monuments in the sacred site such as the temple of Zeus and the Metroon. The whole period is marked by the influx of important spiritual people to the sacred area of the Altis and also by an over-abundance of buildings and offerings which were flooding it.

Herodes Atticus

Herodes Atticus (AD 101-177), the eminent Athenian rhetorician and philosopher, is historically known mainly as a great benefactor and embellisher, not only of Athens but also of other cities. His fabulous wealth and social status gave him the opportunity to develop a multilateral action for public benefit and connections with Roman Emperors (mainly Hadrian and Antonius Pius), and to obtain high-level political titles. He became market inspector and the eponymous dignitary of Athens. He was the head of the committee which welcomed the emperor Hadrian, as well as prelate, consul and editor (emperor's delegate) in Asia. A great part of his life was spent travelling and his large construction works and donations are especially well known. In addition to the famous Odeon of Herodes Atticus which he built in memory of his wife Regilla in AD 161, he also restored the Panathenaic stadium in AD 140, making it marble and giving it an impressive propylon. He built the Nymphaeum at Olympia, which became the water reservoir of the sanctuary, met the expenses of the stone seating for the spectators in the stadium at Deplhi, made donations to the sanctuary of Apollo Isthmios etc. Herodes Atticus was also a distinguished and important rhetorician with a very rich collection of works. However, he was soon forgotten and of these works only a small amount of information survives. The last years of his life were spent in his parents house in Marathon, where he died.

After the death of Alexander the Great, the radiance of the sanctuary began to decline and in 312 BC, it was destroyed by the Macedonian, Telesphorus. During the 3rd and 2nd centuries BC, however, important leaders and rich individuals continued to send offerings and a special significance is assigned to the votive offerings from Arcadia, Achaea and Macedonia during this period, as well as those from Asia Minor and Egypt. At this time, the two buildings on the west of the Altis were built which served the needs of the athletes' training: the Gymnasium and the Palaestra, or arena. In 146 BC, Greece came under the control of the Roman Empire and conceded them the right to take part in the Olympic games which were considered Greek in origin. The sanctuary suffered significant plundering during the Mithridatic Wars and in 85 BC, during the siege of Athens, Sulla plundered the sanctuary and removed a significant amount of treasures from Olympia. In apparent support of this catastrophe, there was the terrible earthquake of 40 BC which caused serious damage, mainly to the large Temple of Zeus. However, during the years of Augustus Octavian (30 BC - AD 14), the sanctuary enjoyed a renewed prosperity and during the reign of Nero, the Olympiad of AD 65 was held two years later in AD 67, so that the emperor himself could take part. He won a number of events, many of which were unknown until then, Nero himself introducing them into the Olympic programme. In the first half of the 2nd century AD, the emperor Hadrian especially favoured the development of the sanctuary and in the latter half of the same century, Herodes Atticus built the Nymphaeum. From the 3rd century AD, the glory of the Olympic games began to decline steadily and the participation of athletes from the various Greek towns became less and less. At the same time, many athletes from the provinces of the Roman Empire expressed their interest in the games and began to take part in the events. The destruction of the temples and other buildings of the sanctuary began in the second half of the 3rd century AD. In AD 267, the Eleans built a wall to confront the invasion of the Herulians using many architectural parts from the temples and buildings which they demolished. Their goal was to protect the Temple of Zeus and its chryselephantine statue within. The invaders did not eventually attack but the life of the sanctuary had reached its end.

THE BYZANTINE PERIOD

In the 4th century AD, the Olympiad had no more religious or political role to play and the last Olympic games took place in AD 393. In AD 394, the Byzantine Emperor Theodosius I issued a decree whereby every 'pagan' festival was prohibited; the games were abolished, the Temple of Zeus fell prey to Christian fanaticism in AD 426 and, as the result of a decree issued by Theodosius II, it was set on fire and destroyed. During the 5th century AD, a Christian community settled down on the banks of the Cladeus river and built a three-aisled early-Christian basilica on top of Pheidias' workshop. The destruction of the sanctuary was finally completed by two terrible earthquakes in AD 522 and 551. From then on the ruins were gradually covered by a layer of mud, five to seven metres thick, as a result of the subsidence of the Hill of Cronus and the flooding of the Cladeus and Alpheios rivers. Under this deep landfill, the ruined monuments remained protected from the plundering of later years until the excavations in this area which began in the 19th century.

MORE RECENT TIMES - THE EXCAVATIONS

The valley of Olympia and its treasures have been the subject of research since the 18th century. Many lovers of antiquity as well as archaeologists wanted to discover the birthplace of the most glorious and famous games of antiquity. From 1723, the Frenchman, Montfaucon, made the first attempts for the beginning of excavations in Olympia but without success. Later, in 1767, the German archaeologist Winckelmann was interested in the survey of the area. The first rough excavations began in May of 1829 and were undertaken by Blouet and Dubois of the French Expédition Scientifique de Morée. The first systematic excavations, however, took place in the years from 1857 - 81 by the German Archaeological Institute under head scientists like Adler, Dörpfeld and Curtius, the expenses being met by the German State. Research began again in 1936 - 41 and continued from 1958 - 61. These excavations brought to light the monuments we see today which testify to the glory of this large religious centre; a meeting place for all Greeks. The research at Olympia continues to this day.

The German archaeologist, Curtius.

3

A TOUR OF THE ARCHAEOLOGICAL SITE

A DESCRIPTION OF ALL THE ARCHAEOLOGICAL MONUMENTS INSIDE AND OUTSIDE THE SACRED ALTIS

The Palaestra.

When the visitor approaches the archaeological site, he meets the bridge over the Cladeus river. Immediately after the bridge, in a peaceful location between the confluence of the Cladeus and Alpheios rivers and the Hill of Cronus, are the monuments of ancient Olympia.

From the first moment it became obvious that the monuments had suffered severe damage which was completed by the two earthquakes of the 6th century AD, and there are many buildings of which only the foundations survive. The most common material used in the construction of the buildings was a coarse local fossiliferous limestone which could be found in plenty in the surrounding area. The buildings which survive today belong to different periods — the site is a real open-air museum — and even ruined show the unique character of the Olympic sanctuary.

A low surrounding wall with three entrances separated the sanctuary from the rest of the site. Our tour will begin from the present-day entrance to the archaeological site and the buildings located to the west of the Altis.

1. Gymnasium
2. Palaestra
3. Greek Baths
4. Swimming Pool
5. Theokoleon
6. Pheidias' Workshop
7. Roman Guest House
8. Leonidaion
9. Prytaneion
10. Philippeion
11. Heraion
12. Nymphaeum of Herodes Atticus
13. Altar of Zeus
14. Pelopion
15. Temple of Zeus
16. Altis
17. South Baths
18. South Stoa
19. Bouleuterion
20. Metroon
21. Zanes
22. Treasuries
23. Echo Colonnade
24. SE Building
25. Stoa of Agnaptos
26. Aphesis
27. Altar-Eagle
28. Dolphin
29. Statue of Hippodamia
30. East Baths
31. Finishing Line
32. Hippodrome
33. Tribune of the Hellanodikai
34. Altar of Demeter
35. Stadia I, II and III

Plan of the sanctuary of Olympia.

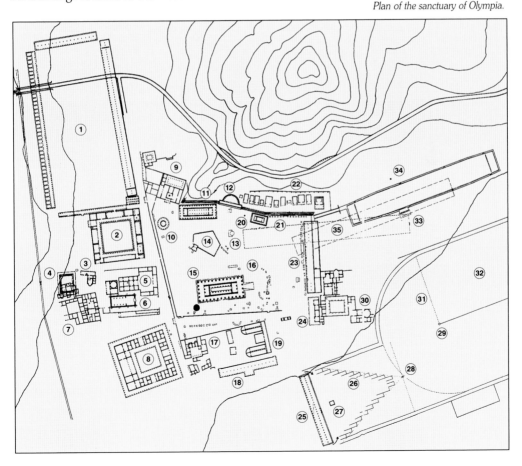

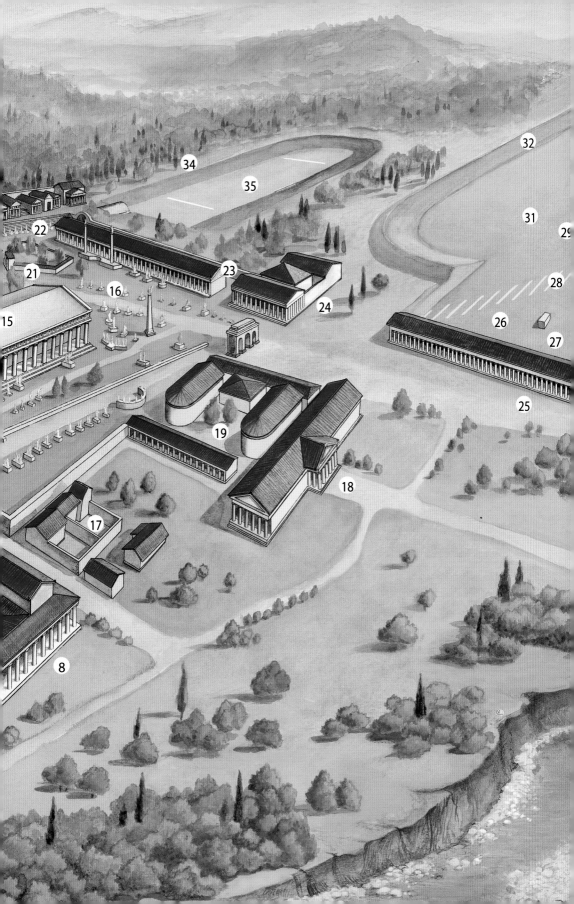

THE GYMNASIUM

The Gymnasium.

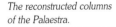

T he first building the visitor comes across on the right is the Gymnasium. It was an enclosed rectangular building with four stoas of Doric style which flanked a spacious central yard, the 'Plain of Ares'. The yard itself has dimensions of 120 x 220 metres and of the four stoas, the eastern and southern ones remain. The building was used for the training of the athletes and mainly for events like javelin, discus and the foot race. The eastern stoa, the *xystos*, housed a stadium 192.27 m in length (exactly one Olympic stade) and was used for training the athletes, mainly in foot races, when the weather was bad. It consists of a double gallery with intermediate and side colonnades. The southern stoa of the Gymnasium survives in its largest part and is dated to the 2nd century AD. At the end of the same century, at the southern end of the eastern stoa, a monumental Corinthian propylon with two internal colonnades was built. This colossal entrance, exactly opposite the north gate of the Altis, connected the Gymnasium to the Palaestra and of this very specially attended monument, survive its foundations along with some of the capitals and a number of drums from the columns. Inside the Gymnasium were a large number of statues of athletes.

THE PALAESTRA

I mmediately after the Gymnasium, to the south, is the Palaestra, or wrestling school. It was built in the 3rd century BC and was used for practicing and the training of the athletes in the events of wrestling, boxing and jumping. The Palaestra had a square plan with dimensions of 66.35 x 66.75 metres and consisted of a central peristyle yard, without roof, surrounded by Doric stoas suitable for the athletes to train in when it was raining. Behind the stoas were various rooms, such as the *ephibion*, where the athletes took lessons from the gymnasts; the *elaiothesion*, where they were rubbed with oil; the *konisterion*, where they were rubbed with sand and other waiting areas which were equally suitable for the speeches of philosophers and rhetoricians. On the northern side was an area with a floor, made of fluted tiles, measuring of 24.20 x 5.44 metres. The room with the tank in the northeastern end was used as a cold bath.

The Palaestra had a central entrance in its northwestern end and the external walls were stone-built in the lower parts and brick higher up.

THE THEOKOLEON

South of the Palaestra, the visitor meets the Theokoleon or Priest's House. It is a rectangular building with a number of rooms surrounding a central yard which was used as the headquarters of the Theokoloi; the priests of Olympia and their assistants. It is dated to between the 5th century and the first half of the 4th century BC. In the Altis, every sanctuary had its own staff headed by three priests, the Theokoloi, who looked after the sanctuary and were also responsible for the main sacrifices.

THE HEROON

The building to the west of the Theokoleon is the 'Heroon' or hero's tomb, according to the late Hellenistic inscription found there during excavations. It was a four-sided building of which, in its northern part, a circular room with an altar has been excavated enclosed within a square wall. It has been proposed that this building was initially a hot bath and was later converted into a temple to honour a hero or heroised dead man. It has been dated to the fifth century BC.

Pheidias' workshop with the area of the Theokoleon in front.

The Workshop of Pheidias

To the south, after the Heroon and the Theokoleon, are the remains of Pheidias' workshop. This building of the fifth century BC, in which Pheidias made the chryselephantine statue of Zeus, had the same dimensions as the cella of the large Temple of Zeus. In this way the artist was able to judge the impression the huge work would give in its natural environment.

In the auxiliary areas of the workshop, various tools of iron, bronze, bone and lead were found along with remnants of ivory, glass ornaments, terracotta moulds and sherds of Attican pots which helped to date the chryselephantine statue of Zeus precisely. The most significant find, however, was the small earthenware pot on the base of which the sculptor had himself carved the inscription: "ΦΕΙΔΙΟ ΕΙΜΙ", I am [the property of] Pheidias.

Later, the workshop of Pheidias was used as a storage for clothes, oil pots, perfumes and in general for all objects connected with the statue. It was also used as a residence of the 'Phaidryntai', the clerks responsible for the upkeep of the statue. In the middle of the 5th century AD, the building was demolished by the Byzantines who built a three-aisled early-Christian basilica on top of it.

The interior of Pheidias' workshop which was later transformed into an early-Christian basilica.

Bath Complex of the Cladeus River

Continuing west, the visitor encounters the remains of the hot baths complex close to the Cladeus river. The oldest part is dated to the 5th century BC and consists of baths and a pool of dimensions 24 x 16 m. The baths were first extended in 300 BC and a second alteration was carried out in the 1st century BC. South of this building, excavations have brought to light remains of a building of the 2nd century AD which may have been used as a residence for the officials from Rome.

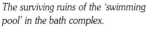

Representation of the bath complex on the Cladeus river.

South Hot Baths

East of the Leonidaion are the remains of the 3rd century AD South Hot Baths, close to the defensive wall of the same period which was built for the protection of the area, primarily the Temple of Zeus, from the invasion of the Herulians.

In the immediate vicinity, remains were found of two houses also of the 3rd century AD.

The surviving ruins of the 'swimming pool' in the bath complex.

LEONIDAION

Around 330 BC, at the southwest corner of the sacred Altis, a very large building was constructed of which today only the foundations survive. Its construction was financed by the architect Leonidas of Naxos from whom it took its name, and its purpose was to accommodate the officials from abroad.

The Leonidaion was probably a two-storey building, almost square in shape, measuring 80.18 m x 73.51 m. It consisted of a central yard surrounded by a Doric colonnade of 44 columns along the inner-facing sides. A number of rooms also looked into the yard. The whole building was surrounded by an Ionic colonnade of 138 columns. In the Roman period, around AD 150, a tank and a garden were built in the centre of the yard. At this time, the Leonidaion was converted and ceased to be a guest house but became the residence of the regional Roman dignitaries.

Top: View of the Ionic colonnade which surrounded the imposing guest house of Olympia, known as the Leonidaion.
Bottom: The Leonidaion.

BOULEUTIRION

In the southern part of the sanctuary and north of the South Stoa, the visitor can see the Bouleutirion. It is a peculiar building which consists of four parts of different construction phases. The Bouleutirion is made up of two apsidal wings, one to the north and one to the south, between which was there was a square open area. The north building was built first, in the 6th century BC and later, around 490 - 450 BC, the south building was added parallel to the north and the open square. During the Hellenistic period the eastern side of the whole building was completed with a large stoa with Ionic façade. In the later Roman period an irregular shaped yard with a Doric peristyle was added to the Ionic stoa.

The two apsidal wings of the Bouleutirion were the headquarters of the Olympic Council, the members of which came from the aristocracy of Elis. They were responsible for the management of the sacred ceremonies, in which they were assisted by a *boulographer*, and held authority over all Olympic officials. In these buildings all official documents and files connected with the games were kept and all cases of contravenance of the rules were judged here.

In the open square there was an altar and the statue of *Zeus Horkios* where, after the sacrifice of wild boar, the contestants would vow to uphold the rules of the games.

The Bouleuterion.

SOUTH STOA

The southern border of the sanctuary was made up of the South Stoa which was built in the middle of the 4th century BC and faced the Alpheios river. On its façade it had a Doric colonnade which was set around a small propylon in the middle of the stoa and continued to the ends. The role of the projecting hypostyle section in the middle of the stoa has not been identified with certainty, but it may have been used as a market place or possibly was one of the official entrances to the sanctuary.

PROCESSIONAL WAY

Along the west wall of the Altis was the Processional Way. It was given this name due to the fact that the procession of the priests, officials, athletes, the Hellanodikai (or chief judges of the games) etc. passed along here on their way to the Temple of Zeus to conduct the ceremonies of the Olympic Games. Around AD 60, Nero built a triumphal apse at the end, but today only the foundations survive. For the whole length of the Processional Way there were, here and there, bases for stelae, like the one of consul Metellus Macedonicus (143 BC) and the equestrian statue of Mummius and of the ten Roman consuls (146 BC).

THE SOUTHEAST BUILDING

At the southeast corner of the Altis, before entering the sacred precinct, the visitor will see the Southeast Building. Built at the end of the 5th or beginning of the 4th century BC, it was originally the sanctuary of Hestia. In the 3rd century BC it was expanded to the east and in the 1st century AD it was demolished. On its foundations a peristyle villa was built of brick to accommodate Nero during his visits to Olympia.

OCTAGONAL BUILDING - EAST HOT BATHS

Next to the Southeast Building are the remains of the Octagonal Building close to the area which was devoted to the worship of Artemis from the middle of the 5th century BC and which has an altar to the goddess. The octagonal building was a Roman building from the time of the Antonines (2nd century AD). Close to this there are also the ruins of the East Hot Baths which were built in AD 200.

The Processional Way.

The South Stoa.

THE TEMPLE OF ZEUS

I n the more central area of the Altis are the remains of the largest temple in the Peloponnese and unquestionably the most important monument at Olympia, the Temple of Zeus. The temple was begun in 470 BC and completed in 456 BC, and was paid for with the spoils taken by the Eleans after the destruction of Pisa in 472/71 BC, as mentioned by Pausanias.

Pausanias also gives us the name of the architect of the temple, informing us that he was from Elis and that his name was Libon. The construction material used was the local coarse fossiliferous limestone which was quarried on the banks of the Alpheios river. This was then coated with white stucco and colours to give the impression that the temple was made of marble. In comparison to this, the pediments, metopes and roof tiles of the temple were all constructed from a white coarse grained Parian marble. In later repairs, Pentelic marble was also used.

The temple was built on top of an artificial hill and dominated the surrounding area with its imposing presence such as could be expected from so important a god. It was a Doric peripteros with 6 x 13 columns and

The Temple of Zeus.

Top: Representation of the eastern façade from the Temple of Zeus at Olympia.
On the pediment are shown the preparations for the chariot race between Pelops and Oenomaus.
Bottom: The western façade of the Temple. On the pediment can be seen the battle between the Centaurs and the Lapiths.

measured 64.12 x 27.70 m with a total height of 20.25 metres. The columns were 10.35 m tall and had a basal diameter of 2.25 m. On top of the columns rested the entablature with architraves 5 metres long and 1.77 metres tall and on top of these stood the triglyphs and metopes. The metopes around the outside were initially undecorated. Only the ten metopes of the eastern side and the eleven metopes of the southern side received twenty-one gilt shields in 146 BC, which the Roman general Mummius ordered to be made from the spoils won after he defeated the Achaeans and conquered Corinth. Resting on the frieze was the horizontal cornice and above this was the sima which had lion-head spouts along its length down the sides of the temple and painted anthemia (flower-like ornaments) at either end.

The central akroteria were the work of the sculptor Paeonius and the corner ones were bronze cauldrons; everything was gold-plated. The temple had an east-west alignment and a ramp led up to its entrance.

In the pronaos and opisthodomos of the temple, there were two columns 'in attendance'. On top of the architrave here, the frieze was decorated with triglyphs and six metopes. Also in the pronaos were many votive offerings such as the horses of Kyniska and the sculpture of Iphitus who was crowned by Ecechiria.

Before the entry to the pronaos, on the right there was a small area which, during the Roman period, was floored with colourful tiles. Here, on the day when the crowns were awarded during the Olympic games, a gold and ivory table was placed upon which lay the crowns of wild olive with which the victors would be adorned. The cella of the temple was divided by two two-storey Doric colonnades into three aisles, the middle one being wider than those on either side. On top of each of the side aisles there was a gallery which the devoted could reach by way of wooden ladders and from where they could admire the chryselephantine Zeus.

The gigantic statue of the god was placed on a pedestal at the end of the cella and was protected by railings one metre high. The pedestal itself was made of black marble from Eleusis and in front of it was a shallow square tank, lined with light-blue marble tiles and surrounded by Pentelic marble into which, according to Pausanias, poured the oil with which the 'Phaidryntai' anointed the statue.

The statue of the god was placed inside the temple after 438 BC and has been characterized as one of the Seven Wonders of the Ancient World. It was so large (seven times life-size) that, according to Strabo, if the god were to rise from his throne, he would unroof the temple. It had a height of 12.40 metres including the pedestal and was made of gold, ivory and other precious materials. Of this masterpiece of classical art, however, nothing survives. Representations of it are possible thanks to Pausanias' description and to Elean coins of the Roman period (2nd century BC) which show, on the obverse the head of Zeus and on the

Image of the Chryselephantine statue of Zeus which was considered to be one of the Seven Wonders of the Ancient World.

reverse the statue. To construct the statue Pheidias worked along with his collaborators, the painter Panainos and the sculptor Colotes. There was also an inscription at the feet of the statue which proclaimed that it was the work of Pheidias, son of the Athenian Charmedes.

The god sat on an impressive throne and was crowned with a golden olive wreath. In his right hand he held a chryselephantine Nike and in his left a sceptre with an eagle on top, the symbol of his power. The throne was made of bronze, gold, ebony, ivory and precious stones and decorated with painted and relief mythological representations. On the upper part it was decorated with the Charites and the Horai, and further down Nikes, sphinxes with young men from Thebes and a depiction of the murder of Niobe's children by Apollo and Artemis. Also shown were athletes, the battle of the Amazons and the birth of Aphrodite.

The skeleton of the statue was wooden, onto which the artist had masterfully attached the gold sheets and ivory. The naked parts; the chest, the feet and the stomach, together with the face, were made of ivory. The hair, beard, sandals and the himation were made of gold. The himation itself came down from his shoulder and fell on his thighs covering his legs. It was covered with precious stones and decorated with zodiacs and lilies. It was said that the statue was so perfect that Pheidias asked the opinion of the god who agreed sending a lightning bolt on the temple without destroying anything. Where the lightning bolt struck, a bronze urn was placed. The statue was in the temple until AD 395 when it was transported to Constantinople where, according to the historians Zonaras and Kedrinos, it was burned during a large fire in AD 475.

Unquestionably the sculptures which decorated the temple belong to the masterpieces of ancient Greek sculpture from the so-called 'severe style'. On the eastern pediment, the preparations for the chariot race between Pelops and Oenomaus was shown, and on the western one was the Centauromacy (the battle between the Centaurs and the Lapiths during the wedding of Pirithous and Deidamia). The twelve metopes which adorned the ends in the external frieze of the cella depicted the twelve labours of Heracles. These sculptures, of which quite a number have been restored, were made by a rather unknown artist, conventionally called 'the Artist of Olympia'.

In front of and around the Temple of Zeus were many votive offerings and works by famous artists, which were offered mainly by rich individuals and various city states and of which, today, only their bases survive. Examples of the kind of art which was present are: the chariot of Gelon by the sculptor Glaukias, the chariot of Hieron by the sculptor Kalamis, and others. Also, close to the south side of the temple grew the sacred wild olive tree from which branches were used to make the crowns of the winners and next to which was the altar of the Kallistephanes Nymphs.

The surviving ruins of the Temple of Zeus.

The toppled columns from the southern part of the Temple.

View of the temple being under reconstruction.

THE PEDASTAL OF THE NIKE OF PAEONIUS

An especially important offering was the Nike of Paeonius. Built on a nine-metre tall, inscribed, triangular pedestal, it stood infront of the entrance to the temple and was a votive offering from the Messenians in 421/20 BC.

a. The pedestal from the Nike of Paeonius to the southeast of the Temple of Zeus.
b. An artist's impression of the Nike of Paeonius on its pedestal.
c. Votive inscription from the Messenians and Naupactians after their victory at Sphacteria in 425 BC. In smaller letters can be seen the signiture of the sculptor, Paeonius of Mendi.

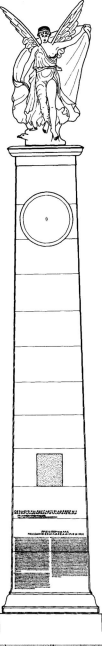

α.

γ.

ECHO COLONNADE

Pedestal from a votive offering.

North of the Southeast Building and opposite the entrance to the Temple of Zeus, The Echo Colonnade was built shortly after 350 BC during the years of Phillip II. It is also called the Hepta-echo (or Seven-echo) and the Stoa Poikile (or Painted Stoa). The first name derived from its special acoustics — it was said that a voice resounded seven times — whilst the latter name came from the murals which decorated the inside.

The stoa had dimensions of 97.81 x 9.81 metres, an external Doric colonnade and an internal colonnade of the Ionic order. At its northern end the contests for the heralds and trumpeters were held. The stoa opened directly onto the Altis and along the length of its entrance were erected various statues. Around the middle of the 3rd century BC, the monument of Ptolemy II Philadelphus and his wife Arsinoe was built. It consisted of two Ionic columns on top of which were placed the gilt statues.

The Echo Colonnade.

THE HIPPODROME

B etween the Southeast Building and the Echo Colonnade was an ancient entrance which led to the Hippodrome. Nothing today survives of the Hippodrome because of the floods of the Alpheios river which have washed it away. It took its final form during the Classical period and representations of it are possible thanks to the detailed description by Pausanias. It had artificial earthwork embankments to the south and east, whilst in the west it ended in the stoa of Agnaptos which, naturally, has not survived. The Hippodrome had a total length of 4 stadia (or 780 m) and in it were held the chariot races and horse races, which belonged to the most glorious of Olympic sports. At the eastern end, around which the chariots turned during the races, was the altar of the demon Taraxippos who was supposed to frighten the horses because, according to myth, the horses of Oenomaus bolted at this place. During the Classical period, a very impressive mechanism (or aphesis) was introduced which controlled the start of the chariots and the riders in a very fair way.

The Hippodrome was separated down the middle by a low wall, at the western end of which was the bronze statue of Hippodamia.

Silver coin depicting Nike crowning the horses of a chariot.

Pot showing a four-horse chariot.

THE KRYPTE - THE STADIUM

After the Echo Colonnade comes the official entrance to the Stadium, the Krypte. It was built in the Hellenistic period (3rd century BC) as an arch-roofed passage which led to the Stadium. At the end of the Krypte which faced the Altis was a propylon with Corinthian columns. After passing through the Krypte, the visitor will see the Stadium stretching out before him. The stratigraphical excavations carried out have distinguished five separate periods —from the Archaic to the end of the Roman— across which the Stadium was built and modified. However, the Stadium that can be seen today is Stadium III from the end of the Classical period (4th century BC).

The Archaic Stadium (Stadium I), was laid out in the area between the Great Altar of Zeus and the end of the Stadium we see today. It was built in the middle of the 6th century BC and lacked the usual embankments. Later, at the end of the 6th or beginning of the 5th century BC, the Stadium was shifted slightly to the east (Stadium II). As excavations have shown, during the 4th century BC the stadium was removed from the sacred area of the Altis and then moved further to the east (Stadium III). In the free space created as a result of this move, the Echo

Opposite at Top: View of the stadium at Olympia. In the background on the left is the altar of Demeter Chamyne and on the right the headquarters of the Hellanodikai.

Bottom: The Krypte.

The Krypte

The Hellanodikai

The Hellanodikai were elected by lot many months before the Olympic Games began and were responsible for the general direction and supervision as well as the correct organization of the Games, and for the enforcement of all rules. In the beginning, there was only one but later the Hellanodikai numbered twelve. Their number was eventually brought down and defined as ten from 384 BC. Their main duty was to impose penalties connected with breaches of the regulations, such as the late arrival of the athletes, bribery and the violation of the rules. An appeal against their decisions was possible in front of the Elean Boule, but this happened very rarely because there were regarded as incorruptible and impartial.

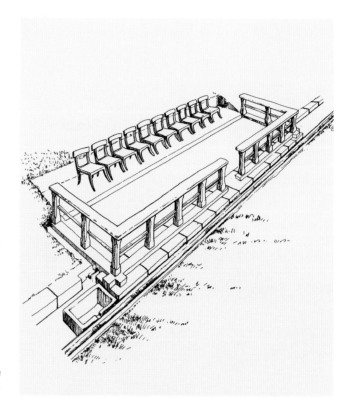

Reconstruction of the platform of the Hellanodikai.

Opposite at Top: The platform of the Hellanodikai on the southern bank of the stadium.

Bottom: The stone altar of Demeter Chamyne on the northern bank of the stadium.

The stone starting line of the stadium which permitted up to twenty runners to start at the same time.

Colonnade was built and many offerings were placed. The width of the track is 30 metres and the length, from start to finish, 192.27 m (600 ancient feet), a distance which, according to the myth, was set by Heracles measuring with his feet.

The start of the tracks was defined by two lines of marble plaques with gutters along their whole length where the feet of the runners were placed, and by squared holes in which the stakes, necessary for the start, were placed. The end had an equivalent arrangement and was also used as a start for the diaulos (two lengths of the track) and the dolichos (or long distance race). The total length of the Stadium was 212.54 metres. On its embankments there were no seats for the spectators who could reach 45,000 people. On the southern embankment was a platform where the ten Hellanodikai sat. Immediately opposite, on the northern embankment, there survives the stone altar of *Demeter Chamyne* where, on a special seat, sat the priestess of the goddess, the only female allowed to watch the games. Around the edge of the track there survives the stone water conduit with basins from which the spectators could drink during the games. Small changes were carried out on the Stadium during the Roman period (1st century AD and 2nd - 3rd century AD), during the last of which, wooden seats were built for the spectators.

THE TREASURIES

On a terrace, at the foot of the Hill of Cronus, are the remains of the Treasuries. The visitor coming out from the Krypte will see them on his right-hand side. They are small temple-like structures with two columns on the façade and are dated to the 6th and 5th centuries BC. They are called treasuries because in them were kept the valuable votive offerings from the various cities.

Pausanias mentions their owners: the Carthaginians, Syracusans, Samians, Epidamnians, Byzantines, Sybarites and Cyreneans. Today, only five have been identified with certainty, those of the Sicyonians, Selinians, Metapontians, Megarians and the Gelans (from west to east). Of the rest, only the foundations survive.

The treasury of the Gelans was built in two phases. It was constructed around 600 BC and later, around 491 BC, a Doric peristyle was added. In the treasury of the Sicyonians, an inscription was found. Finally the richest, as regards external decoration, must have been that of the Megarians, sculptures from the pediment of which survive showing the Gigantomachy, along with parts of the terracotta Laconian roof. To the west of the terrace of the Treasuries was also the sanctuary of the goddess Eilithyia and of her son Sosipolis.

The terrace with the surviving remains of the Treasuries.

THE ZANES

At the foot of the terrace of the Treasuries are the bases of the Zanes, bronze statues of Zeus. The total number of them was sixteen, all paid for by the penalties imposed by the Hellanodikai. They were placed infront of the Krypte so as to make an example of those athletes caught cheating.

THE METROON

Also at the foot of the terrace of the Treasuries, below that of the Sicyonians, was the Metroon, a temple devoted to the worship of the Mother of the Gods, Rhea or Cybele. Today it survives only to the height of its pillar bases as its architectural parts were used in the construction of the 3rd century AD wall which was built to confront the Herulians. The Metroon was a peripteros of the Doric order, with six columns at either end and eleven along the sides. It measured 20.67 x 10.62 m, was 7.50 metres tall and had a stone entablature with limestone columns.

A seated Dionysus probably came from its pediment. In the Roman period, the Metroon was transformed into a temple to Augustus and the other Roman emperors. A colossal statue of Augustus Octavius and later statues of other Roman emperors decorated its cella.

The pedestals of the Zanes.

View of the Metroon from the terrace of the Treasuries.

THE NYMPHAEUM OR 'EXEDRA'

This monument was built between AD 157 and 160 with the expenses of the rich philosopher and rhetorician from Marathon, Herodes Atticus and his wife Regilla and was the water reservoir for the sanctuary. In the Nymphaeum the pipelines ended which transferred the waters from the springs in the villages of Mouria and Miraka. The building consisted, in its upper level, of a semicircular tank where the water was collected. From there it was channeled, via lion-headed spouts, into a long narrow basin with two small circular structures, one at either end, which was on a lower level. From here the water travelled to all of the buildings in the sanctuary via a system of terracotta pipes.

The higher tank was surrounded by a two-storey semicircular apse with niches in which there were statues of Antoninus Pius and his family, offered by Herodes, along with fifteen statues of Herodes and Regilla and other members of their family which the Eleans had offered. In front of the semicircular tank had been erected a marble statue of a bull with a votive inscription by Regilla.

The Nympheum of Herodes Atticus. This work was of enormous benefit to the sanctuary of Olympia, especially during the Games when it swarmed with thousands of visitors.

Opposite at Top: The marble bull from the Nympheum with the votive inscription by Regilla who offered the entire building, together with the sculptured decoration, to Zeus during the year when she carried out the duties of the priestess of Demeter. The inscription says "Regilla, priestess of Demeter, the water and the surrounding water of Zeus"

Bottom: View of the Heraion from the east. In front is the altar of Hera and to the right can be seen the surviving remains of the Nympheum.

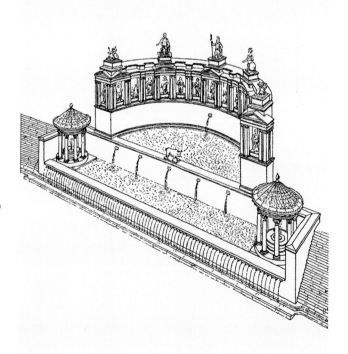

Reconstruction of the Nympheum of Olympia.

THE HERAION

Southwest of the Nymphaeum are the remains of the Heraion, one of the oldest Doric temples in Greece. Its first construction phase is dated to the middle of the 7th century BC, but its present style is from around 600 BC. The first small temple, with only a pronaos, occupied the space taken up by the present-day cella. This was later extended and was completed with an opisthodomos and a surrounding wing of wooden columns. The temple in its last phase was a Doric peripteros with six columns on the ends and sixteen along each side. Its measured 50 x 18.75 metres and had a height of approximately 7.8 metres

The cella was long and narrow and the pronaos had two columns between the ends of the side walls (or antae). The opisthodomos was divided by a wall from the main chamber and also had two columns between the antae. The cella itself was divided by two colonnades into three uneven aisles. Between every second column and the walls of the cella were walls set at right angles which thus

The Heraion.

formed rectangular niches. The lower part of the cella walls were made of the local fossiliferous limestone whilst the upper parts were of unbaked brick. Of the entablature no stone architecture survives and it is therefore thought to have been wooden. The roof was covered with Laconian terracotta tiles and the top of each pediment was crowned with a huge 'disc like' terracotta akroterion.

The columns of the temple were initially made of oak and measured 5.22 m in height. Their replacement with stone columns was carried out over many centuries, as and when the deterioration of the wooden ones made it necessary. This progressive replacement of the columns resulted in the fact that the style of the capitals, and the number of flutes and drums, depended entirely on the decorative trends of the particular period in which the column was replaced. The evolution of the Doric column, and especially of the capital, can therefore be seen in this temple from the Archaic period (a crown-shaped capital) through the Classical period (a capital with ridges) up to the Roman period (capital with echinus). Pausanias mentions that in the 2nd century AD there was still one column made of wood.

At the end of the cella were the statues of Hera, seated on a throne, and of a bearded Zeus standing next to her wearing a helmet. Of these statues, only the head of Hera survives. The niches of the cella were adorned with various statues and it was here that the famous sculpture of Hermes and Dionysus by Praxiteles was found. Also in the Heraion, the disc of Iphitus with the text of the Sacred Truce was kept along with many other valuable objects such as the urn of Cypselus, made of cedar wood and decorated with various mythological designs; the gold and ivory table by Pheidias' student Colotes, where the crowns of the winners were placed etc. During the Roman period, a large number of sculptures, mainly of Elean noble women, by Athenian artists, were placed in the pronaos.

A specially-formed stairway at the northwest edge of the temple led to the Gaion, the most ancient sanctuary of Gaia at the foot of the Hill of Cronus.

The limestone head of Hera, the only thing that has survived of the colossal seated statue of the goddess. Dated to around 600 BC, it is one of the earliest examples of the Peloponnesian plastic arts in stone. (Archaeological Museum of Olympia)

THE PELOPION

To the south of the Temple of Hera are the remains of the temenos of Pelops. Its original structure, dated to the Geometric period, consisted of a simple perimeter wall surrounding a small enclosure. Later, during the 6th century BC, this simple wall was replaced by a pentagonal one and, in the southwest, a propylon was built which became more monumental during the 5th century BC. In the centre of the enclosure was the altar of the hero, his statue and a pit where a black ram was sacrificed every year in his honour.

THE GREAT ALTAR OF ZEUS

Southeast of the Heraion was the Great Altar of Zeus of which nothing survives. It was surrounded by a stone wall, was approximately seven metres high and had been formed from the accumulated ashes of the sacrificed animals from the hearth of the Prytaneion (with the eternal flame). However, the mound was scattered by wind and rain when the sanctuary was abandoned. Every year the priests would cover the altar with clay which they formed from water of the Alpheios river and ashes from the altar of the goddess Hestia in the Prytaneion.

Between the Altar and the Temple of Zeus, Pausanias mentions that there was an inscribed column from the ancient palace of Oenomaus.

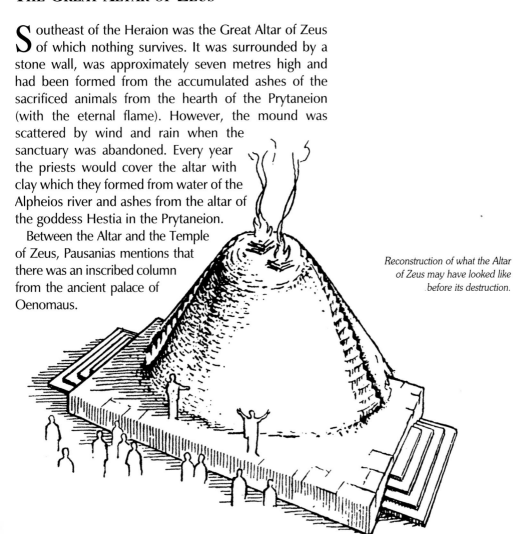

Reconstruction of what the Altar of Zeus may have looked like before its destruction.

THE PHILIPPEION

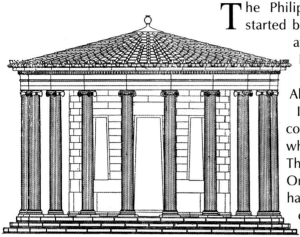

Artist's impression of the Philippeion.

The Philippeion, south of the Heraion, was started by Philip II of Macedonia a short time after the battle of Chaeronea in 338 BC. Philip died in 336 BC, however, and the building was finished by his son, Alexander the Great.

It is a circular building with 18 Ionic columns in the peripteros, or perimeter, which had a diameter of 15.24 metres. The roof was conical with marble tiles. On the interior wall were Corinthian half-columns and on the side of the chamber opposite the entrance was a semicircular marble pedestal with finely crafted mouldings. On this were placed five chryselephantine statues by the famous sculptor Leochares. These were of Philip, his wife Olympia, his parents Amyntas and Eurydike, and his son Alexander. None of these statues have survived.

The Philippeion.

The Prytaneion

In the northwest corner of the altis is the last building the visitor will come across before leaving the sanctuary; the Prytaneion. It was built in the 5th century BC and was the headquarters of the officials of the sanctuary. In this building, celebratory gatherings and formal dinners were held for the officials and winners during the Olympic Games. It was a complex building with a special area in the south which housed the altar of the goddess Hestia, with the eternal flame which burned day and night. It was here that the Eleans made their sacrifice on the first day of the Games. The Prytaneion had a peristyle yard and many rooms which were used as auxiliary areas. There were also kitchens and tavernas where the official guests and Olympic winners were hosted during the games and where the priests and the servants ate during the rest of the year. The Prytaneion was the political centre of the sanctuary and was, excavations have shown, reconstructed and extended many times especially during the Roman period.

The surviving remains of the Prytaneion.

Chapter

4

THE
ARCHAEOLOGICAL
MUSEUM

- Presentation of the Exhibits Housed
in the Twelve Galleries of the New Museum
- Presentation of the Museum of the History
of the Ancient Olympic Games

B288 Bronze protome of a griffin.

All the finds from the excavations carried out at the archaeological site of Olympia are today exhibited in the New Archaeological Museum which was restored in the last decade.

Previously, all of the archaeological treasures had been housed in a beautiful neoclassical building designed by the German architect, Dörpfeld, and situated very close to the small town of ancient Olympia. The old museum was begun in 1886 and funded by the national benefactor, Andreas Syngrou. However, the continuance of the excavations resulted in an ever-increasing number of finds and the need to find a new place in which to house the whole exhibit. In addition, the earthquakes of 1954 had caused quite extensive damage to the building which was difficult to repair. All of this led to the construction of the new museum which was completed in 1975, (with the opening ceremony being held in 1982). The new museum is set in a verdant landscape on the north side of the Hill of Cronus and the collections are exhibited in chronological order in its spacious galleries.

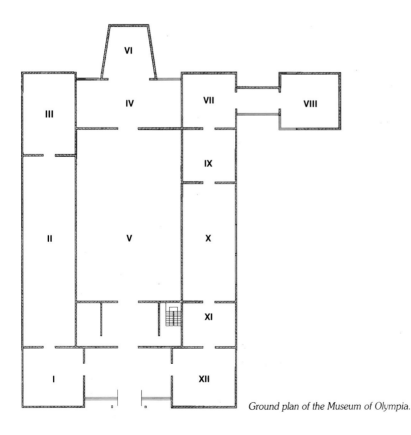

Ground plan of the Museum of Olympia.

GALLERY I - PREHISTORIC EXHIBITION

Most of the exhibits in this room belong to the Mycenaean period (1600 - 1100 BC) and more specifically to the late Mycenaean (1425 - 1100 BC). During this time, the whole of the Peloponnese witnessed a great prosperity. The oldest finds in the room are dated to the early Helladic period (the beginning of the 3rd millenium BC), whilst the more recent ones represent the late Mycenaean period up to the end of the 12th century BC. The numbering of the display cases is from left to right making it easier to follow the chronological sequence.

CASE 1

This Case contains finds dating from the Late Neolithic until the LH III period from the region of Olympia. These finds provide evidence that the area was inhabited from as early as 4,200 BC. There are also finds from apsidal buildings II, III, V and VI of the Altis, the Sacred Precinct of Zeus.

In particular, fragments from the Late Neolithic, sections from EH I "fruit bowls", fragments of the LH II period, cauldrons, "salad bowls", inscribed cups, phials, kantharoi and amphora of the MH period, as well as obsidian blades and various stone tools are exhibited.

CASE 2

In Case 2 we can see finds from infant inhumations in pithos jars found in the Sacred Precinct (askoi jug, grey Minyan kanthar without handles, pithos burial jars) and finds from the recent excavation of 1989 at the "altar" of the large tumulus of the Pelopion (single- and double-handled phial, small bronze chisel, censer, etc.). There is also typical pottery of the EH III and MH I periods from the Altis, MH I-II pottery and various prehistoric tools from the Stadium (various grey Minyan vessels, fragments of dark brown pottery, tools, stone axes).

CASE 3

In Case 3 are exhibited finds from the Mycenean tombs around the area of the new Museum of Olympia, in particular from the Zouni chamber tomb, from a series of chamber tombs of the Kalosaka group as well as from other Mycenean sites around Olympia. From the Zounis tomb are exhibited a female figurine with arms raised, an alabaster, a spherical

stirrup jar and clay or steatite spindles.
From tomb B of the Kalosaka group are exhibited
clay spindles, an alabaster and small alabasters,
handle-less spherical jars, glass jewellery, small
amphorae, kyanthoi with ring handles, as well as
a bronze leaf-shaped razor and a bronze spear tip.
There are some finds from chamber tomb H
of the Kalosaka group, such as various stirrup jars,
alabasters, spindles, bowls, kylikes and necklace
beads of glass, faience and horn. There are similar
finds from chamber tomb I and the tomb from the
1972 excavation of the Kalosaka group.
Particularly impressive are the kyanthoi with ring
handles, the bronze leaf-shaped razors and the
spherical alabaster with its foot taken from a kylix.
From chamber tombs 1, 2, A and pit grave I
of the Kalosaka group are exhibited small pithos jars,
glass necklaces, fragments of a kylix and spindles
of clay and steatite.
Finally, from chamber tombs B, D, F, G, H and I
of the Kalosaka group and from other Mycenean sites
at Olympia there are small round stirrup jars, small
alabasters, kylikes, steatite seals as well as a headless
transitional type female idol. Case 3 concludes with
finds from the Submycenean period: these are
a section from a large conical kylix and ribbed
stemmed conical kylikes.

Page 68a Stirrup jar.
Page 68b Three-handled small pithos jars.
Page 68c Section of a one-handled phial.
Page 69a Assyrian sheets.
Page 69b Pear-shaped pithos jars.

CASE 4
Here we can see bronze Assyrian hammered sheets.

GALLERY II - PROTOGEOMETRIC, GEOMETRIC AND EARLY ARCHAIC PERIODS

The main exhibits in this room are bronze finds dating to the Protogeometric and Geometric periods (10th – 8th centuries BC) as well as the Archaic period (7th – 6th centuries BC). During these centuries offers were made to Zeus, in his character as the warrior, of every kind of weapon. Notable are the helmets, especially the Corinthian and Illyrian ones, the shields, breastplates, swords, spearheads etc., many of which have rich engraved decoration. The greaves, from the area of Olympia, show excellent workmanship in their manufacture and their shape is adapted to fit the form of the leg. Also in this period, were offered ankle-guards, thigh-guards, armguards and almost every type of defensive weapon in bronze.

B1670

B4

B28

B5

CASE 1

Bronze and terracotta figurines of people and animals and other bronze objects which decorated the handles of cauldrons. These are votive offerings left in the Sanctuary by the faithful, and which date to the Geometric period. They were found in the thick layer of ash that had covered a large area around the altar of Zeus.

CASE 2

In this Case one can see a large number of clay votive figurines that were found in the area between the Heraion and the Pelopion in the Precinct. The figurines are mainly of animals, but they also represent male and, more rarely, female figures. Also exhibited here are bronze figurines and votive tripods. The great majority of these works are from Peloponnesian workshops, dating from the 9th to the 7th centuries and represent male and, more rarely, female figures. The microscopic tripod cauldrons can mainly be placed in the Geometric period. Particularly impressive here is the group of four small bulls (9th century BC) as well as the group of seven women performing a "circle" dance. In the same Case we can also see bronze figurines from the Geometric and Archaic periods (horse and bull figurines, warrior figurines that were used as decorative cauldron handles). Especially noteworthy here is the solid cast horse, singular in its monumentality, as well as the group of three dogs attacking a deer. Finally, bronze sheets dating to the Geometric period are also exhibited.

CASE 3

In the third case in this room the visitor can see a bronze cauldron that is dated to the late 8th century BC. It once bore attached to its rim five bull heads on which had been carved the inscription, in the alphabet of Elis, "IAPON ΔIOΣ" (Iaron Zeus).

CASE 4

This Case includes parts from bronze vessels attached either to the rim or the handles and which date to the 7th-6th centuries. There are also animal figurines, warriors, bullheads and also characteristic figurines of the fighter and the old man (B5000 and B25). Also on exhibition are bronze sheets from the Archaic period such as the Gorgon, a shield bearing, sheets with the figure of a Sphinx, another with the figure a cock, etc. The female mask from a Laconian workshop that once adorned the wooden statue of a female divinity is particularly impressive (B5099).

B2610

B6500

B2610 Bronze helmet of the 'Corinthian' style.
B1670 Bronze figurine of a charioteer on his chariot.
B28 Bronze winged figure, the handle of a cauldron from the end of the 8th century BC.
B5099 Hammered bronze female mask from the second half of the 7th century BC.
B4990 Bronze official shield with a representation of a demonic figure, possibly Phobos, from the 6th century BC.
B6500 Female winged demonic figure of hammered bronze from the beginning of the 6th century BC.

CASE 5

In this Case the visitor can admire a large, well preserved tripod cauldron in the typical style of the Geometric period.

CASE 6

In this Case are exhibited parts from bronze defensive armour. In particular, a sheet with a winged horse, a sheet with a winged Gorgon, a shield bearing, a bronze Illyrian helmet, the only one decorated with silver sheets, as well as an impressive winged Gorgon (B110) that has been hammered and with incised details.

CASE 7

Here we can see bronze helmets dating primarily from the Geometric period. The majority of these are helmets with specially formed coverings for the nose and the cheeks. The earlier, conical helmets are also of interest.

TO THE LEFT OF THE EXIT

Colossal limestone head of the goddess Hera, the statue of which was in the Heraion beside a statue of Zeus (Λ1). This work is dated to the beginning of the 6th century BC. In the rest of the built-in display cases are exhibited various bronze sheets and also figurines, which are dated to the 7th - 6th centuries BC.

CASE 8

This Case contains parts of bronze defensive armour from the 7th to 6th centuries BC, such as greaves, armour for arms and forearms and mitres to protect the groin area. There is also a reconstruction of an Archaic shield and shield "holders" decorated with relief representations, as well as a bronze shield decoration made from hammered sheets and with the figure of a cock (6th century BC).

CASE 9

In this Case are exhibited the back section of a bronze breastplate. It bears engraved decoration with mythological representations, such as the liberation of Helen by the Dioscuri after her kidnap by Theseus and Perithoos.

B5000

B5101

B25

CASE 10

In this Case is exhibited a number of military votive offerings, most of which were found in the Sanctuary and which often feature interesting decoration.

CASE 11

This Case presents another large number of Geometric tripod cauldrons, typical of the so-called "orientalising" style.

CASE 12

Archaic bronze sheets are exhibited in this Case. These include a sheet dating to the second quarter of the 7th century BC that had possibly been adapted to a particular architectural member, the lower section of a sheet with a palmette, sheet depicting a dragon attacking a wild goat and a sheet with two centaurs. The sheet with representations on metopes (M77) depicting Orestes killing Clytaimnestra whilst being egged on by Electra stands out, as does the kidnap of the Amazon Antiope by Theseus (ca 580 BC). This Case also features the monumental bronze sheet (B104) with a female griffin suckling her newborn, as well as bronze busts of "monumental" size griffins.

CASE 13

A bronze orientalising-style cauldron is exhibited in this case. Its conical stand is characteristic, as are the facing male figures and the depiction of a lion.

B104

B5000 *Bronze figurine of a warrior.*
B5101 *Bronze breast plate.*
B25 *Bronze figurine of an old man.*
B104 *A female griffin feeding her young. Of particular note is the affection and directness of the terrifying figure, and the severe lines of the topic the sculptor has created.*

CASE 14

In this Case we can see bronze animal figures from cauldron rims (griffin busts and a lion bust, winged male and female figures, etc.) as well as bronze figurines from the handles and other parts of cauldrons (legs, handles). These finds date from the 8th until the early 7th centuries.

Π2969

Π2969 The central terracotta akroterion from the Heraion.
M77 Bronze sheet with relief decoration in three parallel zones. Orestes killing Clytemnestra under the encouragement of Electra (middle zone). Theseus kidnapping the Amazon, Antiope (lower zone).
B1240 Bronze tripod cauldron (9th cent. B.C.)

CASE 15

In this case we can admire bronze Geometric tripod cauldrons as well as other cauldron parts, dating from the second half of the 8th century BC.

CENTRAL CASE

Hammered bronze sheet showing a female griffin feeding her young, from a Corinthian workshop of the first half of the 7th century BC. This work shows how Greek art tamed the demonic figures of the East, showing them in a more naturalistic style.
Also on exhibition is a large hammered bronze lion's head, with engraved details and which was probably part of the building's architectural decoration.

JUST BEFORE THE EXIT

At the end of the room there is a section of a terracotta akroterion from an unidentified building, possibly a treasury. which is dated to the third quarter of the 7th century BC.

74
M77

B1240

GALLERY III - ARCHAIC PERIOD

The third room of the Museum of Olympia is basically a continuation of the second, because here are also exhibited finds and architectural elements from the last phase of the Archaic period. Of interest is the black-figure pottery of the period as well as elements of the decoration of the Archaic buildings in the Altis which are exhibited in this room.

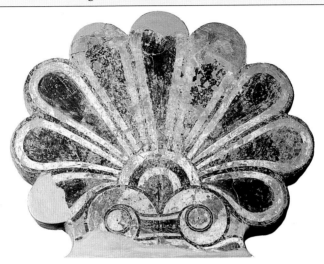

CASE 1

Terracotta pots of the 7th and 6th centuries BC. Most of them are black-figured and their colours have survived to the present. In the same display case are also a series of pots from the first half of the 5th century BC.

CASE 2

Parts of bronze cauldrons and other vessels. Remarkable are the legs of incense burners, the lion feet from tripods and a very well preserved bronze basin. Also on exhibit are handles from bronze vessels and other bronze decorative parts, as well as bronze vessels and jewellery, the most characteristic being the palmette handle crowns, the similar moveable Archaic handles, the palmettes on the upper curves of tripods, various human and animal figurines, parts of vessels, as well as a cut-out sheet featuring the head of a female figure.

THE TREASURY OF THE MEGARIANS

On display at the end of the room is the entablature, together with the pediment, from the Treasury of the Megarians.
The sculptures on the pediment, from the 6th century BC, are made of limestone and show the Gigantomachy (the war between the gods and the giants). The inscription 'ΜΕΓΑΡΕΩΝ' ('MEGARIANS') on the architrave, is from the Roman period.

TO THE RIGHT OF THE EXIT

A section of the clay painted decoration of the pediment of the Treasure of the Gelans is displayed here, with wonderfully preserved colours, thanks to the excellent technique used.

Section from the clay painted decoration of the pediment of the Treasury of the Gelans.

The **Treasuries** follow the form and shape of small temples. They are found in large Sanctuaries, having been constructed by the Greek cities, in particular the colonies. They were probably originally used for worship, and were later used to store the valuable votive offerings that the cities had dedicated to the Gods.

The Treasuries at Olympia were built on the natural terrace formed at the foothills of Mt Kronos. Pausanias records the names of ten Treasuries although the remains of twelve buildings survive here. The Treasury of the Megarans (above figure) most likely had the richest decoration, whilst a Doric persityle was added to the Treasury of the Gelans (figure below) during a later building phase.

Reconstruction of the entablature with the pediment of the Treasury of the Megarans.

T1

CASE 3

In this Case we can admire pottery from Elian, Corinthian and Attic workshops, as well as clay human and animal figurines. The exhibits include black-figure lekythoi, Archaic female figurines, measuring vessels and drinking vessels from local workshops. Particular attention should be paid to the clay head of a Siren (T1) from the corner ornament of the Treasury of the Gelans (520-530 BC), a small "Elian" pear-shaped amphora decorated with facing horses and a "Corinthian" kothon drinking vessel with painted decoration of Sphinxes.

CENTRE OF THE ROOM

A limestone lion is exhibited in the centre of the Room (Λ3), which was probably used as a gutter on a fountain. It is dated to 680-670 BC and is one of the earliest works of monumental sculpture to have been found in Greece.

K1292

K1292 Laconian kylix depicting Hera and Zeus seated on thrones. In the background can be seen the eagle, symbol of Zeus (Around 530 BC).

T1 Clay head of a Siren from the corner ornament of the Treasury of the Gelans (520 - 530 BC).

77

GALLERY IV - CLASSICAL PERIOD

It is known from the sources that, during the golden era, the area of the sacred Altis was swamped with works by outstanding craftsmen; large sculptures or groups of sculptures, terracotta statues, votive offerings for buildings and others, which were offered by various cities, rich people or victors in the games. Unfortunately, due to the disruptions and plundering of the following periods, only a few pieces have survived in their entirety.

CASE 1

In this Case are exhibited sections of large clay sculptures used as corner decorations on Archaic buildings. These include sections from sculptures of Winged Nike and a Sphinx, whilst items TC3529 and TC1048 (K172), sections from a clay group featuring the persecution of Maina by a Satyr are of particular interest.

CASE 2

Terracotta group of Zeus and Ganymede. According to the myth, Zeus fell in love with Ganymede and abducted him from the area of Troy. He then led him up to Olympus and made him the cup-bearer to the gods. This group represents the precise moment of the abduction. Zeus holds his knotted travelling staff and Ganymede holds a cockerel which symbolizes the element of love. The group stands on a peculiarly shaped base. Quite a number of the colours have survived: the dark blue, the chestnut brown on the eye brows of Ganymede and the hair of Zeus, the pale yellow of the bodies and the dark red. The sculpture survives to a height of 1.10 meters and contains a number of Archaic characteristics in the representation of the heads and the hair. The work comes from a Corinthian workshop and is dated to around 470 BC.

CASE 3

Two inscribed helmets (M9 and M844), a Corinthian and Etruscan one. Both are offerings from the tyrant of Syracuse, Hieron, after his victory in the naval battle of Cyme against the Tyrrhenians (Etruscans) in 474 BC.

CASE 4

The next two helmets on display are equally as important. The one may have belonged to Miltiades, the Athenian general who beat the Persians at Marathon in 490 BC, and has the inscription "ΜΙΛΤΙΑΔΗΣ ΑΝΕΘΕΚΕΝ ΤΟΙ ΔΙ", which means "Miltiades presented this to Zeus". The second

helmet, of bronze, is conical and may be Assyrian. It has the inscription "ΔΙΙ ΑΘΕΝΑΙΟΙ ΜΕΔΟΝ ΛΑΒΟΝΤΕΣ" indicating that it is part of the Athenian spoils taken from the Medes during the Persian wars which was later offered to Zeus.

CASE 5

In a display case on a tall base is exhibited a small bronze horse (B1000), the only one to have survived of the quadriga (four-horse chariot) to which it belonged. It is dated to 470 BC approximately.

CASE 6

Bronze figurines of Zeus with the lightning bolt in his right hand along with statuettes of Athena, Hermes and the goat-like Pan. Ringlets and parts of statue legs are also on display.

CASE 7

Here we can admire bronze vessels from the Classical period, such as oil lamps, a deer figurine, oinochoe, phials, etc. There is also a large number of bronze weights, of which the star-shaped weights and those weights bearing the inscription "ΔΙΟΣ" (Zeus) stand out.

B2600

T2

CASE 8

An important clay statue of a warrior is exhibited in this Case (T3). It was made in a Peloponnesian workshop and belonged to a votive group, the other figures of which do not survive (ca 480 BC).

CASE 9

In here is exhibited a bronze battering ram, a votive from the Sanctuary. It dates to the mid-fifth century BC. This was siege weaponry and it bore sculpted relief decoration of a ram's head at each end. Possibly the work of a Sicilian workshop, this is the only battering ram to survive from this period.

CASE 10

The bronze bullhorn and ear in this Case are particularly impressive. A work of the bronze sculptor Philesios, its was a votive offering from the Eretrians after their victory against the Athenians at the beginning of the 5th century BC. In the base of the votive is the inscription "ΦΙΛΕΣΙΟΣ ΕΠΟΙΕΙ ΕΡΕΤΡΙΕΙΣ ΤΩ ΔΙΙ' (Philesios made this for the Eretrians to Zeus).

CASE 11

Head of a terracotta statue of the goddess Athena, dated to 490 BC approximately. The expressiveness of the face is a characteristic element of the 'severe style' (first quarter of the 5th century BC).

B1000

CASE 12

In the last Case in this Room (right of the entrance) we encounter a clay reclining lion from a Corinthian workshop (mid-5th century BC), probably an offering to the Sanctuary, as well as a clay dolphin jumping out from the waves. This dates to the end of the 5th century and probably decorated the sima of a circular building.

T3

B2360

GALLERY V - THE SCULPTURES FROM THE TEMPLE OF ZEUS

The Central Room of the Museum hosts one of the most impressive works of art from the early Classical period; the pediments and metopes from the Temple of Zeus. The sculptures belong to the so called 'severe style' and must have been created and put in place by 456 BC. It is a miracle, the number of pieces of the 42 figures from the pediments wich have survived and were found during the German excavations of the last century. Most of the information we have on the subject of the pediments comes from Pausanias. In his text he describes them in detail and also mentions the artists. The east pediment he attributes to Paeonius of Mende and the west to Alcamenes. This information, however, does not seem to fit with the style of these two artists, nor with the chronological facts.

Today all researchers do not accept the false information put forward by Pausanias concerning the craftsmen of the sculptures at Olympia. Together with the 'Artist of Olympia', as the creator of the sculptures is conventionally known, there must have been many skillful hands working in collaboration during the sculpting as well as in the finishing touches. This would have consisted of a workshop or school directed by an artist, himself obiously influenced by the monumental painting flourishing at the time and also willing to experiment in the possibilities of an art whose new functions, especially in the representation of the expressions of realism, had begun to develop and become known.

Unquestionably, without the mass of marble sculpture from Olympia, we would be deprived of some of the most important works of all time and, at the same time, a measure of comparison without which it would not be possible to judge the achievements of the Classical technique which followed. Some of the figures of the pediment survive in their entirity, others only in fragments. Their reconstruction in the museum was based partly on the descriptions given by Pausanias and also according to their height which increases from the corners to the centre. Many difficulties were encountered and many possible solutions presented themselves for the placement of the two couples on the east pediment because Pasusanias mentions "right" and "left" of Zeus without clarifying whether he means right and left from the god's or the visitor's viewpoint. The representation shown in the museum today is based on scientific research carried out by N. Gialouris and which is considered to be the most accurate. The restored pediments and metopes are missing the bronze objects; the chariots, weapons and, in general, all items of equipment belonging to the figures, which would certainly have been used in antiquity to strengthen the impressive ensemble. In addition, only a few traces of colour have survived, mainly on the eyes and hair of some of the figures, in relation to the rich colours which would have been used to adorn the statues.

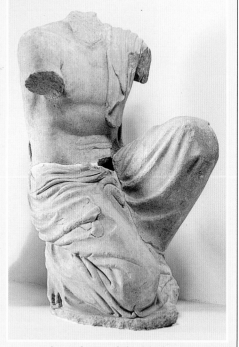

A seated servant behind the four-horse chariot of Oenomaus. (East pediment)

Opposite: The west pediment.

EAST PEDIMENT

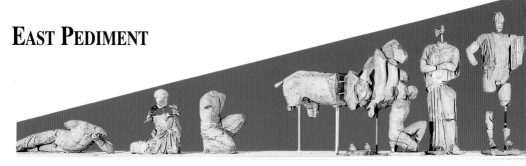

Depicted on the east pediment are the preparations for the chariot race between Pelops and Oenomaus.

Λ50: In the centre of the composition stands Zeus who, as an invisible presence, watches the contest. In his left hand he was holding the lightning bolt (or a sceptre). The head of the figure has not survived.

Λ51: On the right of Zeus (left as the visitor looks) is Oenomaus, king of Pisa. In his left hand he held a spear whilst he rests his right on his waist. His whole posture emits the certainty of his victory.

Λ60: Next to Oenomaus stands his faithful wife Sterope. With her arms folded in front of her, she seems very thoughtful and concerned.

Λ56: Behind Sterope and infront of the quadriga, is a kneeling man who may be Oenomaus' charioteer Myrtilus.

Λ54 and **Λ55**: The quadriga of the king follows and after it the seated servant of Oenomaus.

Λ57: Another male figure follows which may be the seer Iamos or, according to others, Klytios, the founders of the two hieratic tribes from which the priests of Olympia originated.

Λ58: The last figure, which completes the left corner of the pediment, is a personification of the Cladeus river.

Λ59: On the other side of Zeus stands Pelops. He held a spear in his right hand and a shield in his left.

Λ52 and **Λ63**: Next to him stands Hippodamia, who wears a belted Doric peplos and lifts her

Λ52-Λ63-Λ61

Λ64: Finally, the right corner ends with a recumbent figure; the personification of the Alpheios river. The existence of the two rivers in the corners of the pediment indicates the area in which the games were held, which is defined by the Cladeus and the Alpheios — Ancient Olympia.

The composition on this pediment is static, the figures do not move and are full of tension awaiting the fatal contest. Despite the fact that the faces are isolated, there is a general atmosphere of communication and participation in the air. This shows particularly in the central figure group whose axes are vertical, whilst the symmetry of the others contrasts just a little because of the different positions of the kneeling figures and the horses.

dress in a gesture appropriate to a bride. At her feet and infront of the quadriga of Pelops, is a kneeling maidservant.

Λ61: Next are the four horses with the chariot which may have been bronze.

Λ62: Beside it sits a thoughtful old man, the seer (possibly Amythaon). His sad expression, with his hand supporting his head, and the pain he emits, sum up the tragedy of the moment and the foreboding of the dramatic end.

Λ53: Behind him sits a young man playing idly with his fingers. He has been identified as the hero Arkadas as he resembles the depiction of this hero on the Arcadian coins.

WEST PEDIMENT

On the west pediment the battle between the Centaurs and the Lapiths is shown. According to the myth, Pirithous, king of the Lapiths and friend to Theseus, married the daughter of Adrastus, Deidameia. In order to honour the wedding, he invited the Centaurs as relatives of the Lapiths (the two tribes had the same descendant, Apollo). During the reception, the Centaurs got drunk and, led by Eurytion, tried to kidnap the beautiful Lapith women. A terrible battle followed and the Lapiths, with the help of Theseus, chased the Centaurs off for their lack of respect to the sacred law of hospitality.

Λ65: In the centre of the pediment stands Apollo. In his left hand he held a bow whilst his right was stretched out protectively over Pirithous. The god, magnificent and calm, is the avenger of the insult and comes to restore right and order. The movement of his arm reveals that the outcome of the battle had been judged in favour of the Lapiths.

Λ68: On his right is Pirithous, who holds a sword and is ready to attack the Centaur, Eurytion.

Λ67 and Λ66: The latter, next to him, has grabbed Deidameia and is holding her around the waist with his right arm and clutching her breast with his left. Deidameia tries to defend herself and escape from his violent embrace. The wildness and the crudity on the face of Eurytion contrasts vividly with the beauty and sweetness of Deidameia — it is one of the most beautiful groups of the pe.

Group of a Centaur and female Lapith (Λ81 and Λ82).

The Centaur Eurytion and Deidameia (Λ67 and Λ66).

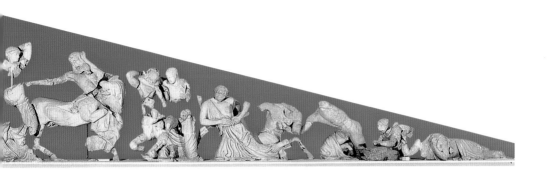

Group of a Centaur and female Lapith
(Λ84, Λ83 and Λ85).

Λ70 and Λ69: Another group follows where a Centaur is grabbing a young boy.

Λ72, Λ73 and Λ71: Continuing, we come to a Centaur who has seized a kneeling female Lapith by the hair while, at the same time, a young Lapith attacks him and brings him to his knees.

Λ74 and Λ75: Finally, the left corner of the pediment (as the visitor looks) ends with two female Lapiths who, frightened, are lying down watching the fight.

Λ80, Λ78 and Λ79: Left of Apollo (right as the visitor looks) is Theseus who holds a sword or axe in his raised hands and is ready to attack the Centaur who is next to him and has taken a Lapith woman. The woman, trying to escape,

pulls the hair and beard of the Centaur with all her might. The intensity on the face of the Centaur shows his anger and the pain the Lapith woman has caused.

Λ82 and Λ81: Next is a group consisting of a Centaur and a male Lapith. The Lapith grasps the head of the Centaur and tries to strangle him while the latter bites him hard on the arm.

Λ84, Λ83 and Λ85: Continuing, there is a female Lapith who tries to push away a Centaur who is grabbing her by the waist and her leg while a male Lapith stabs a knife into his chest.

Λ76 and Λ77: The composition is completed again, in the right corner with two cowering Lapith women who, full of fear, are watching the fight. Of these four corner figures, only the first from the right is made of Parian marble, the rest are of Pentelic marble and may be later additions created when the originals fell off the pediment due to strong earthquakes. Two new elements have been introduced into the sculpture on the west pediment: intense motion and expression. In contrast to the east pediment where the figures, motionless and isolated, await the tragic end, on the west pediment the battle is at its peak. The heroic attitude towards the animalistic offensive behaviour is evident; it is the complete conviction of the insult with a divine assistance. The subject was widely used in art of the 5th century BC and intensely paralleled by the victories of the Greeks over the barbarians.

The Apples of the Hesperides

The dog, Cerberus, from Hades.

The Augean Stables.

THE METOPES

In the central room can also be seen the twelve metopes from the Temple of Zeus. They were arranged six above the internal colonnades at either end. The metopes, of which Pausanias mentions all but one, show the twelve labours of Heracles and are the first representation of them. The presence of Heracles here is not difficult to explain being, as he is, the son of Zeus and mythical founder of the Olympic games. The metopes have a height of 1.60 metres and a width of 1.50 metres and some are very fragmentary with many pieces having been removed to the Louvre after the French excavations of 1829. On the six metopes from the opisthodomos, from left to right, the first six labours of Heracles are depicted:

METOPE I *Heracles is shown, on the first metope, holding the sky while Atlas brings him the golden Apples of the Hesperides. Athena, dressed in a Doric peplos, uses her left hand to help Heracles lift the vault of the heavens.*

METOPE II *On the second metope Heracles drags the terrible dog Cerberus from Hades. Behind him stands Hermes who accompanied Heracles on his descent to Hades and also on his return.*

METOPE III *On the third metope, Heracles is shown cleaning the Augean stables. Athena, next to him, indicates to the hero, with her spear, where he should dig in order to make the waters of the two rivers, the Alpheios and Pineios pass through and clean the stables*

The Cretan Bull of Knossos.

The Ceryneian Hind.

The Girdle of Queen Hippolyta.

The Stymphalian Birds.

The Lernaean Hydra.

The Nemean Lion.

METOPE IV *Heracles hands over the Stymphalian Birds to the goddess Athena, who wears an aegis and sits on a rock.*

METOPE V *Heracles slays the Lernaean Hydra. Only a few fragments of this metope have survived.*

METOPE VI *Heracles is shown young and clean-shaven resting after slaying the Nemean Lion. Athena watches him affectionately and is encouraging him, whilst behind him is Hermes. This composition showing the exhausted hero is a pioneering work and we see it again only as engraved representations on jewellery.*

METOPE VII *Heracles tames the Cretan Bull of Knossos. The robust intersection of the axes forming the bodies of the hero and the bull, emit an intensity and dynamism.*

METOPE VIII AND METOPE IX *On the eighth metope, Heracles tames the Ceryneian Hind and on the ninth metope he kills the amazon Hippolyta.*

METOPE X *On the tenth metope, Heracles kills the three-bodied demon Geryon.*

METOPE XI *On the eleventh metope, Heracles tames one of the Horses of Diomedes. The pioneering mood of this composition is noticeable from the intersection of the two main axes, the hero's and that of the horse, in the shape of a cross.*

METOPE XII *On the last metope, Heracles hands over the Erymanthian Boar to Eurystheus who cowers, terrified, in a large pot.*

The Oxen of Geryon.

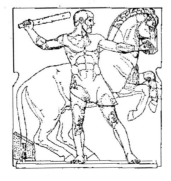

The Mares of Diomedes.

The Erymanthian Boar.

89

 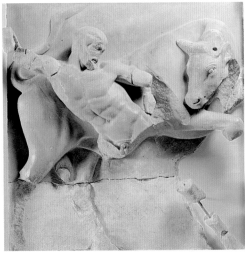

On the metopes, the control of the artist within the square area containing the figures is particularly masterful. The variety of compositional shapes is outstanding: on the first metope showing Heracles with the Nemean lion, the horizontal element stresses the peaceful mood of the hero; on the metope with the Stymphalian Birds, the artist expresses a quirky, lyrical style and on the metope with the Ceryneian Hind, the composition is pyramidal. Of especial pioneering style are the two metopes showing Heracles with Cerberus and Heracles with Athena at the Augean stables where the action is completely balanced by the horizontal elements despite it being expressed t o the corners.

Forerunning and innovative techniques are used on the metopes with the Nemean lion, the Stymphalian Birds and the Augean Stables. Heracles is shown on all metopes, except the first, with a beard and his moods are transparent; reflected in his expressions: tiredness (Met. VII), pride (Met. IV), intense effort (Met. I) and strength and concentration (Met. II).

Above left:
Herakles holds up the sky, whilst Atlas hands him the Golden Apples of the Hesperides.
Above right:
The Cretan Bull.
Below: detail from the above photograph.

Opposite page.
Right: Herakles, from the metope with the Augean Stables.
Left: the young Herakles, from the metope with the Nemean Lion.

Lion-head waterspout from the Temple of Zeus. Of the large number of waterspouts, only four are today exhibited in the museum and it is clear that their artistic value is proprotional to that of the sculptures of the Temple.

WATERSPOUTS

In Gallery V are four of the waterspouts from the Temple of Zeus which were made in the shape of lions' heads. Initially, all the lions' heads were made of Parian marble, but through the centuries, with the severe earthquakes suffered by the region and the sanctuary, it became necessary to replace many of the water spouts which had been destroyed. From 456 BC, when the temple was finished, such replacements had been carried out at least nine times. The latest sculptures are made of Pentelic marble and date back to the 6th century AD when the two catastrophical earthquakes took place.

The typological evolution of the waterspouts and the figure of the lion's head can be seen by studying all the groups and other similar sculptures which have survived from the temple of Zeus.

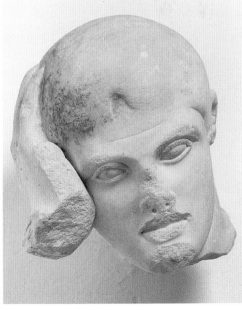

THE NIKE OF PAEONIUS

Here one can see the magnificent personification of Nike. The work is signed by the sculptor Paeonius from Mende in Chalcidice and was created between 425 - 421 BC. The statue is of Parian marble, has a height of almost 3 m and was placed on a triangular base which had twelve drums, of which only six have survived. The pedestal had a height of 9 m and narrowed towards the top. The sculpture was erected a short distance from the southeast corner of the Temple of Zeus and on the front of the third drum from the bottom was inscribed, in 421/20 BC, the following inscription "ΜΕΣΣΑΝΙΟΙ ΚΑΙ ΝΑΥΠΑΚΤΙΟΙ ΑΝΕΘΕΝ ΔΙΙ ΟΛΥΜΠΙΩ ΔΕΚΑΤΑΝ ΑΠΟ ΤΩΝ ΠΟΛΕΜΙΩΝ... ΠΑΙΩΝΙΟΣ ΕΠΟΙΗΣΕ ΜΕΝΔΑΙΟΣ ΚΑΙ Τ' ΑΚΡΩΤΗΡΙΑ ΠΟΙΩΝ ΕΠΙ ΤΟΝ ΝΑΟΝ ΕΝΙΚΑ", meaning, "This work was offered by the Messenians and the Naupactians to Olympian Zeus as tithe for the spoils of war... It was made by Paeonius from Mende who was distinguished as the winner (in a contest) for the making of the akroteria for the temple". The sculpture was, therefore, a votive offering from the Messenians and Naupactians after their victory over the Lacedaemonians at Sphacteria in 425 BC.

Nike, the personification of the victorious outcome of battle, is shown landing, but is still airborne and at her feet is an eagle with outstretched wings. In her raised left hand she holds the thin Doric *himation* (garment) which is blown up behind her due to the strength of the wind, whilst the *chiton* (undergarment) sticks to her body revealing her harmonious physique. In her right hand she once held a crown of wild olive or a branch of palm or laurel and her wings were open during her descent. Of this outstanding sculpture, today survives most of her head, her body and that of

The Nike of Paeonius.

Opposite: A reconstruction in plaster of the Nike of Paeonius.

the eagle. However, the wings of the goddess have not survived, nor have those of the eagle. Neither have the himation or other parts of the peplos, the face of the goddess or her arms, except for a part of her right arm.

The torso of the sculpture has a sharp forward inclination which is balanced by the heavily-pleated himation and the peplos which blow to the back, thus transforming the heavy mass of marble which was needed for the support of the work, and giving to the shape a light, harmonic movement which is still impressive today.

GALLERY VII - THE WORKSHOP OF PHEIDIAS

This new Room, which has been added to the Museum, is dedicated to the greatest sculptor of antiquity, Pheidias, and to his chryselephantine statue of Zeus, one of the seven wonders of the world which was produced at his workshop at Olympia ca 430 BC.

Clay corner tile and section of a palmette end tile
from the Workshop of Pheidias.

Pheidias, son of the Athenian Charmides and a relative of the painter Panainos, demonstrated an early inclination toward painting. He devoted himself, however, to sculpture and had an excellent artistic training with the help of his teacher, who was either Hegias or Ageladas from Argos. He worked in wood, marble, gold, ivory and bronze. Among Pheidias' early works are: a chryselephantine statue of Athens (which he made for the town of Pallene and of which no copies survive), a statue of Apollo (the so-called "Parnops", i.e. pursuer of the locusts) that was set up on the Acropolis of Athens, a statue of the poet Anacreon (a copy of which exists in the Museum of Copnhagen) and the Athena Promachos, a brilliant giant statue set up on the Acropolis near the Propylaia of which it was said

that the golden tip of Athena's spear could be seen from Sounion (the statue had been made with the booty from the battle of Marathon). During this same period, before the greatest phase of Pheidias' work, the chryselephantine statue of Zeus was set up at Olympia. This was a giant statue that represented Zeus seated on a throne adorned with painted and relief decoration and with valuable metals and ivory. Together with its base, the statue reached a total height of 13 metres and the head almost brushed the roof of the temple. This was followed, after 448 BC, by Pheidias' greatest phase of production, when Pericles invited him to create the artistic adornment of the Acropolis and the temple of the goddess Athena, the Parthenon.

Terracotta oinochoe, or wine cup, with the inscription "ΦΕΙΔΙΟ ΕΙΜΙ" on its base.

CASE 5

Bone and ivory tools and objects (chisels, grindstones, etc.) are exhibited in this Case. The tip of a deer horn, used for piercing holes, is particularly impressive. There are also bone decorative objects, such as the palmette leaves.

CASE 6

Clay architectural members from Pheidias' workshop are exhibited in this Case. More specifically, we can see a palmette corner tile, a section of a sima decorated with a painted meander pattern, a lion-head from a gutter as well as sections of a pedimental sima with painted decoration.

CASE 7

In this Case we have clay architectural members from the roof of the Workshop of Pheidias, such as a section of an Ionic pedimental sima, sections of palmette corner tiles, etc.

An imposing painting featuring a reconstruction of the chryselephantine statue of Zeus is exhibited in the centre of the Room. In the statue's base one can see a model of the Workshop of Pheidias.

CASE 1

In this first Case, to the left of the entrance, we encounter clay vessels that were found in Pheidias' workshop. These are drinking cups (kypella, skyphoi, kyanthous), with the most amazing of all being the oinochoe that bears the engraved inscription "ΦΕΙΔΙΟ ΕΙΜΙ", i.e. "I belong to Pheidias". Also exhibited here are fragments of a crater with a representation of Nike and a cithar-player by the painter Cleophon (440-430 BC), as well as oil lamps, tablets and sections of clay vessels.

CASE 2 AND CASE 3

Both Cases exhibit a set of clay pleat moulds from the workshop of Pheidias. Among the most important finds in the Sanctuary, the moulds were used to render the pleats on the upper and lower dress of the statues. They were also used in the creation of the chryselephantine statue of Zeus. In this Case are also exhibited glass decorative items in rhomboid and star shapes as well as palmette leaves.

CASE 4

Here we can see a number of bronze and lead items, most characteristic being the goldsmith's hammer and the double lead axe that was most likely used for processing glass.

Clay pleat moulds from the Workshop of Pheidias.

GALLERY VIII - THE HERMES OF PRAXITELES

This room plays host to the most famous exhibit of the museum which is regarded as an authentic work of the sculptor, Praxiteles. In the 4th century BC, it is possible to distinguish three major personalities in art: Scopas, Lysippus and Praxiteles. In this period the idealistic art gave way to naturalistic anxieties. The 4th century is less peaceful, more mystical and more anxious than the previous one. All the contradictory trends coexist and lead to the total development of realism. Now the idealization of the form is not the aim but the depiction of the real expression and mood. Praxiteles in particular looks for the beauty in tender and often effeminate bodies of young men. He is also an incomparable lauder of female beauty. He is fascinated by delicate figures, with him the gods lose their robustness. His art can be regarded as the eternal search for beauty and the mysticism of his work is clear and has deep platonic influences.

The statue of Hermes who "holds Dionysus as an infant", as Pausanias informs us, is a "work of Praxiteles". The statue came to light during the German excavations of 1877 in the area of the Heraion where it stood. This unique statue was created in Parian marble, had a height of 2.13 metres and is dated to around 330 BC. It shows Hermes as a naked teenager supporting himself on his right foot whilst the left one is bent loosely behind him. With his bent left arm, he leans against the trunk of a tree, where his himation is thrown and holds in his right arm the infant Dionysus, whom he looks at. In his right hand, which is broken off but was raised, he is believed to have held a bunch of grapes, the symbol of Dionysus, with which he provoke the attention of the little one. In his left hand, Hermes must also have held his own symbol, the caduceus, as the position of his fingers indicates.

According to the myth, Zeus assigned Hermes the mission of safe-guarding the young Dionysus, the fruit of his love affair with Semele, from the envy of Hera. Hermes had to transport the infant to the Nymphs who would raise him secretly. On his way, the god stopped for a while to rest and, holding the child in his arms, he was amusing him with a bunch of grapes. It is exactly this moment of relaxation which is represented in the sculpture.

The artist worked with special sensitivity on the young well-proportioned body of Hermes, the features of his face and the folds of his himation. The eyes of Hermes look towards the infant god but his gaze seems to get lost in the horizon. His body has an 'S'-shaped stance and is characteristic of the works of Praxiteles. The appearance of the god with his sweet nostalgic expression, the soft cheeks, the well-built body and the soft, slender and highly-polished skin, represents the robust teenager of the 4th century BC.

The Hermes of Praxiteles was found almost complete during the excavations, but the lower part of the tree and the legs of the god (the right calf and the left leg from the knee down) have been added in plaster. As the evidence of gold plating on the head indicates, Hermes must have worn a golden crown.

GALLERY IX - CLASSICAL AND HELLENISTIC PERIODS

In this Room are exhibited finds from the late Classical and Hellenistic periods from the region of Olympia.

To the left of the entrance we encounter a marble statue of a seated female figure, perhaps the votive offering of a distinguished Elian. At half life-size and with a bird at her right thigh, this is an excellent work of the Roman era.

CASE 1

In this Case is exhibited characteristic late Classical black-figure pottery from the Sanctuary. This pottery features kantharous, craters, "Elian" kylikes, "Elian" skyphoi, etc. Also exhibited is a number of Hellenistic figurines, the most characteristic being the clay statuette of Pan (T160) and the tragic mask. Finally in this Case we encounter usable items from the Classical and Hellenistic periods, such as c lay pots and amphorae decorated with two black-figure bands.

CASE 2

This Case contains sections of stone and bronze statues from the late Classical and Hellenistic periods. Specifically, a bronze statuette of Athena, a headless marble statuette of a resting Herakles, the tip of the right hand from a bronze female statue, the body of a statuette of either Apollo or Dionysus, a headless statuette of Asclepius, etc. are exhibited. Also exhibited in this Case are clay architectural members from the Echo Colonnade, such as the section of a lion-head sima and four palmette corner tiles.

To the left of the exit we encounter the statue of a male figure, most likely identifiable with Dionysus and which adorned the Prytaneion. It is made from Laconian marble and dates to the early 3rd century.

The statues of male and female figures in the later Classical and Hellenistic Room.

GALLERY X - NYMPHAION, ROMAN PERIOD

In this room are exhibited works from the Roman period which, however, have strong echoes of clearly Greek influence in their stylistic characteristics. The majority of the statues shown here are portraits of Roman emperors but there are also statues of various dignitaries. Many of the sculptors where Greeks and this explains why their art follows the hard linear design of the figure which is imposed by Roman art, but which found an outlet for its expression in the softer Greek forms.

Άγαλμα του αυτοκράτορα Αδριανού.

The following works are exhibited on the left-hand side of the Room, beyond the entrance:

Headless statue of a Roman emperor in military uniform, perhaps Marcus Aurelius (AD 161-180). Typical is the relief gorgon on the breastplate, as well as the body of a phoenix by his right leg.

Female statue dating to the Roman period portraying Faustina the Elder, wife of Antoninus Pius, in the large "Herakleiotissa" style.

Female statue in the small "Herakleiotissa" style, most likely a portrait of Faustina the Younger, wife of the emperor Marcus Aurelius. Another interpretation is that this is Athenais, daughter of Herodes Atticus.

Statue of a young woman, most likely portraying either Annia Galeria Faustina or Lucilla, daughters of Marcus Aurelius. The inscription states that the statue of Galeria Aurelia Faustina stood on the same base as the statue of her brother T. Aelius Antoninus.

Head of the emperor Lucius Veres. The other surviving parts suggest that he was represented in military dress.

Corinthian column capital from the Nymphaion.

Headless statue, probably of the emperor Marcus Aurelius in military dress. He may have held a spear in his left hand, whilst on his breastplate there are griffins in relief, above which a western motif can be discerned. It has been suggested that this statue of Marcus Aurelius dates to the later period of the embellishment of the Nymphaion.

Statue of the emperor Hadrian crowned with a laurel leaf. The relief decoration on the breastplate is characteristic, with Nikes crowning a statue of Athena Pallas that stands on the wolf that suckled Remus and Romulus.

Headless statue of a figure wearing a toga, perhaps Herodes Atticus from the Nymphaion (AD 101 - 177).

The following works are exhibited on the right-hand side of the Room:

Headless female statue of either Elpinike, daughter of Herodes Atticus, or Faustina, wife of Marcus Aurelius.

Statue, perhaps of Aetilia Cucida Tertulla.

Headless statue of a toga-wearing Roman, perhaps of Appio Annius Gallus, father of Regilla. By his right leg is a characteristic scrinium.

Headless female statue holding a phial and a libation in her right hand. This is most likely to be Regilla, the wife of Herodes Atticus, or perhaps Elpinike, his eldest daughter.

Statue dressed in a himation, in the style of the Dresden Zeus.

Statue representing the emperor Titus (AD 79 - 81) in military dress. Crowned with an acorn branch, his breastplate features a series of relief representations. His sword is by his leg, leaning against a tree trunk.

Headless female statue, possibly Athenais, granddaughter of Herodes Atticus, or of Regilla's mother A. Caeca Tertulla.

Headless statue, perhaps of Regillus, son of Herodes Atticus, that stood upon the same base as the statue of Athenais.

Head of a bald man, perhaps from the statue of M. Appius Braduas, grandfather of Regilla.

In the centre of the Room is exhibited a marble statue of a bull with a votive inscription in Regilla's name. It had been set up in the centre of the Nymphaion as symbol of the element water, in front of the upper semicircular tank.

The Room with the Roman statues from the Nymphaion.

GALLERY XI - ROMAN STATUES

In this Room are exhibited Roman statues found in the Metroon and the Heraion.

Λ143 Female statue which probably depicts Agrippina the Younger.
The himation with the rich drapery which covers the head identifies the empress as a priestess.

Λ125 Statue representing the emperor Claudius (AD 41 - 54). It is the best preserved of those found in the Metroon.

Λ142 Headless statue of a woman. It probably depicts the empress Domitia, wife of Domitian (AD 81 - 96).

Λ144 Marble statue of a noble woman. It was initially believed to be a representation of Poppaea Sabina, the wife of Nero.

Λ141 Headless statue of a noble woman from Elis, the work of the Athenian Eleusineios (second half of the 1st century AD).

GALLERY XII - LATE PERIOD

This new Room, which has been added to the Museum, contains finds that date from the last phase of the life of the Sanctuary until its destruction in the 4th century AD.

CASE 1

This Case exhibits iron tools used in the Sanctuary of Olympia, such as axes, pincers, scythes and pickaxes.

CASE 2

In Case 2 are exhibited iron harnesses and chains from scales and suspension hooks as well as two interesting bronze horse figurines on which the bridles and reins can be discerned. Also exhibited are iron keys and spits from the Sanctuary of Olympia.

CASE 3

Here we encounter a large number of clay Roman vessels, dating from the 1st to the 4th century AD. Most of them were found in the Leonidaion, which was used as a hostel for distinguished visitors to Olympia. Many more were also found in the Baths that were used by the athletes. These include oinochoe, small amphorae, small oinochoe, salt cellars, skyphoi, cups and cooking vessels. Also exhibited are a clay female head with a diadem, a clay figurine of an ox as well as a gryllos from a workshop in either Elis or Asia Minor. Finally, also worthy of attention are the six bronze ring seals with representations of Sphinxes and divinities.

CASE 4

In Case 4 are exhibited Roman clay vessels as well as Roman clay architectural members. Particularly impressive are the drain in the form of a lion's head from the Leonidaion as well as the section of a sima with a lion's head and two palmette corner tiles with the head of Zeus. In the same Case we can see a series of finds from the Frankonisi Mirakas Cemetery, a site around two kilometres east of Olympia. The close relationship with the Sanctuary of Zeus is attested to by the existence of inscribed tomb stele that belong to athletes who participated in

the Games and were later buried there and also by the tombs in which Sanctuary officials were buried. Exhibits from the Cemetery include clay vessels, such as saucers, perfume bottles, cooking vessels, cups, etc. as well as various grave offerings which, on the whole, come from child burials, such as clay male puppets, bronze jewellery, section of a marble tomb stele, an iron strigil, clay figurines and eight clay spools.

CASE 5

Clay and glass vessels are exhibited. The glass perfume jars and phials were made by blowing the glass, which is transparent and colourless.

CASE 6

In Case 6 we can see a large number of Roman oil lamps, simple vessels that were used as the basic means of lighting. They bear relief or painted decoration, whilst the name of their maker is inscribed on the base. Also exhibited in this Case are clay vessels and bronze jewellery from the early Christian years of the Sanctuary. It was during these years that a Christian basilica church divided into a nave and aisles with an apse was built on the ruins of the Workshop of Pheidias. Finally, there are also clay vessels from the last phases of the life of the Sanctuary, such as handle-less pithos-type vessels that were found used as burial goods in graves and which date to the 7th-8th centuries AD. Much later, a layer of earth around 7 metres thick covered the Sanctuary caused perhaps by flooding of the Kladeos and Alpheios rivers or by landslides from Mt Kronos. Over 1100 years had to pass until the first excavations of the French Expédition de Morée in 1829 for the Sanctuary to be remembered once more.

Glass phial.

MUSEUM OF THE HISTORY
OF THE ANCIENT OLYMPIC GAMES

In the wonderful protected building of the old Museum one can admire a presentation of the history of the ancient Olympic Games. Fully restored, the neo-classical building designed by the German architect Dörpfeld today houses finds that are connected to the history of the Olympic Games and which come from the region of Olympia and the whole of Greece.

Room 1 is dedicated to the "Prehistory of Sport", with works from Minoan Crete and Mycenean Greece, which feature the earliest references to sport. Room 2 relates the "Beginning of the Games" through exhibits representing myths connected to the foundation of the Olympic Games in the prehistoric period, historic times and the age of Homer (Room 2a). Room 3 introduces us to "The Organisation of the Games" and contains bronze and stone inscriptions with catalogues of the chief judges and athletes, rules of the Games for athletes and judges, etc. Room 4 relates the "Preparation of the Athletes" with finds either depicting scenes from the life of the youth in the competition areas or that are directly related to sport (Room 4a).

Characteristic of this thematic unit are the vessels with representations of athletes, the bronze strigils that the athletes used to scrape the oil and dust from their bodies after the Games, and also a bronze discus and a stone halter from Olympia (6th-5th century BC). Room 5 takes a look at "Women's Games", the prohibition of women's participation in the Games, whilst in Room 6, the central Room of the Museum, there is a presentation of the "Programme of the Olympic Games" with statues of athletes and bases inscribed with the names of Olympic victors.

In the next two Rooms, 7 and 8, the presentations are of "Victors - Athletes" as well as their "Trophies and Offerings". The "History of the Olympic Games and the Sanctuary of Zeus" comes to a close in Room 10. Here are exhibited coins with depictions of the Games, tablets and statues of figures who are associated with the period when the character of the Games changed from being local to ecumenical. Rooms 11 and 12 take a look at the "Panhellenic Games" whilst in the final Room, Room 13, there is a presentation dedicated to the "Panathenaia", the most important festival of Athens in the classical period, with finds that come mainly from the Acropolis of Athens.

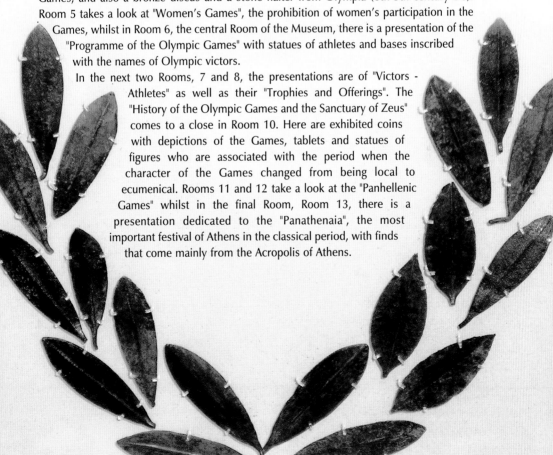

5

THE OLYMPIC GAMES IN ANTIQUITY

- THE RELIGIOUS CHARACTER OF THE GAMES
- HISTORICAL YEARS
- THE ORGANIZATION AND SUPERVISION OF THE GAMES
- THE RITUAL AND ADMINISTRATION OF THE GAMES
- THE HERAIA • THE OLYMPIC EVENTS
- THE OLYMPIC TITLE
- POLITICAL AND CULTURAL CONTRIBUTION OF THE GAMES
- HELLENISTIC AND ROMAN PERIODS:
  THE INEVITABLE DECLINE

*Representation of two naked runners on a Panathenaic
amphora from the middle of the 4th century BC.*

THE RELIGIOUS CHARACTER OF THE GAMES

In the beginning, the panhellenic religious ceremonies which took place in various regions, were carried out for a number of reasons. They were connected with agricultural worship, with ceremonies of germination or with the worship of a god or hero. Also in these religious festivals, the practice of the athletic games was established. The athletes came to the stadium to compete for a self-governing value that came from within them; the athletic ideal, asking also for the help of the gods in their attempt. Their victory was a generous offer to the god. The combination of religion and athletic games went to show that victory was a gift from god and that any kind of violation of the rules of an honest

contest was sacrilegious and an act of blasphemy. The Olympiad, as a religious ceremony, initially had a funereal character. However, with the domination of the Olympic Pantheon, the older worships were set aside.

Representation of a torch bearer, on a red-figured krater of the 5th century BC. (British Museum, London)

In the beginning, the Pisatans were the ones honouring Pelops, the mythical founder of the games, at Olympia but the Eleans later enforced the worship of Zeus. However, close to the Temple of Zeus there remains a place sacred and revered, the Pelopeion, and a black ram was sacrificed there every year in honour of Pelops. This event symbolized the initial funereal character of the games. No other people in antiquity had such a passionate love for sports nor developed the athletic spirit to such a high degree as the ancient Greeks. Their love of competition dominated every aspect of their life and art. They believed very strongly that the sports not only entertained, but that they also exercised the body and mind, thereby contributing to the development of all values.

HISTORICAL YEARS

I n the historical years, after the descent of the Dorians, the games were re-established by Oxylus, leader of the Aetolo-Dorian tribes. Later, however, they were neglected until the time of Iphitus, king of the Eleans, who re-established the games again. From the time of Pelops and Heracles, up to the first historically recorded Olympiad, it has been estimated that the games were not held for 112 years (a total of 28 Olympiads).

The first Olympiad is placed in 776 BC. Then the 'Sacred Truce' was decreed by Iphitus, Cleisthenes of Pisa and Lycurgus of Sparta. With its establishment, the Olympic Games contributed to the cultivation of inter-Hellenic and trans-Hellenic relations, and the strengthening of the bond between the Greek city states. The sanctity of the Games and also of the site where they were carried out, compelled the participants to be free of

Depiction of the 'personified' battle on a tetradrachm of 510 BC (British Museum, London). From the 5th century BC, the Greeks used to depict the fight as a young man with halteres in his hands. A statue of him has been erected in the sanctuary of Olympia.

any hostile intentions and obsessions as they were protected by god. All this atmosphere gave to the Olympic gatherings a religious character and removed everything sacrilegious and profane. As time passed, the Olympic Games became the most important of all celebrations. The athletic spirit became isolated from the worship and developed a completely independent position. Thus, while in the beginning the stadium was part of the sanctuary, in the newer arrangement it was completely cut off from it. The testimony of Thucydides, claiming that the athletes were competing naked during the games, also shows the progressive split of the games away from the conservative spirit of worship and their development into a clean athletic event.

Representation on an amphora, showing an athlete using a strigil to clean his body of the sand and oil that covered it during the games.

The Olympiads were held every four years, at the end of a period which was alternately fifty and forty-nine months long, and which coincided with the eighth lunar month of the Eleans. As a result of this, the games were either in the month of Apollonios (August/September), or in the month of Parthenios (September/October). According to Pausanias, the first thirteen of the known Olympiads from the years 776 - 728 BC, had only one sport: the 'stadion', which was a foot race of one Olympic stadion and had a length of 178 - 179 metres. In the first six Olympiads, the reward was an apple and later a wreath from the 'Kallistephanos olive tree' was awarded. The branch was cut with a golden sickle by a child whose parents were both alive.

During the 14th Olympiad of 724 BC the *diaulos*, a race of two stadia, was added and in the 15th Olympiad of 720 BC, the *dolichos*, a long distance race was added. From the 18th Olympiad of 708 BC, the pentathlon and the wrestling were included. In the 23rd Olympiad of 688 BC, boxing appeared and in 680 BC, in the 25th Olympiad, the chariot race was added as an event and it was only during the 65th Olympiad of 520 BC that the race in armour was included. In the meantime, other sports were added up to 200 BC when the event of the pankration for boys was included into the programme. The Olympic programme was thus constantly enriched and the final form consisted of sixteen events.

Trainer or paedotribis, from
a representation of exercises of the pankration on a red-figured kylix by the 'Artist of Chyterion', from around 480 BC. (British Museum)

Flute player from a depiction of the jumping events. Dated to around 480 BC.

THE ORGANIZATION AND SUPERVISION OF THE GAMES

The Eleans proved to be capable organizers of the Games. The highest dignitaries of the Games were the Hellanodikai, who initially numbered just two and then twelve (one from every tribe of the Eleans), whilst from 348 BC their number was defined as ten. The Hellanodikai, who wore purple robes, were elected by lot from all of the Eleans for each Olympiad and were responsible for organizing the games and the application of the rules. It was within their authority to disqualify individuals from the games because of violation of the rules, and to impose fines or punish those concerned with a public flogging.

In the Altis, every sanctuary had a special staff headed by three Theokoloi for each Olympiad, who conducted the main sacrifices. There were also three *spondophoroi* who were assigned the duty of travelling throughout the Greek world and announcing the celebrations and the Games, as well as seers, descendants of the two oldest families of Elis, the Iamides and the Klytiades. These seers gave prophecies and had a special prestige. There were also priests who conducted sacrifices, flute players, dancers, heads of ceremonies, and others. Finally, the Hellanodikai were helped in their job by the *alytai* (a kind of policemen), the *mastigophorai* (whippers) and the *rabdouchoi* (staff bearers) who answered to the alytarch. Ten months before the beginning of the games, the Hellanodikai stayed in a special building and were informed of their duties. The athletes had to announce to them their participation in the games, one year before they began. With the onset of the Sacred Truce, the believers, official visitors and the athletes swarmed to Olympia. Those who would participate in the Games had to come with their trainers one month earlier in order to prepare themselves and so that all the necessary verifications could be done. That the athletes were of Greek origin was a necessary condition of participation, but the events were open to all free Greeks born of free parents.

Barbarian slaves and all those involved in acts of sacrilege (*i.e.* those who had done something unholy), along with those who had broken the Sacred Truce, and the

Hellanodikai, were all excluded from competing in the Games. During the last month of intensive training, the athletes were taught the principles of the honest game. When this stage was completed, and after they had taken the oath swearing that they had completed ten months of training, a sacrifice and purifying ceremony was performed in the Piera spring.

According to Pausanias, unmarried women were permitted to watch the games. However, married women were prohibited from being spectators and were also not allowed to cross the Alpheios river during the games, the only exception was the priestess of Demeter Chamyne who was allowed to attend. Any violation of this rule was punishable by death. The only instance where this rule was broken and the death sentence not carried out was the case of Kallipateira, daughter of the Rhodian, Diagoras, who came to the stadium disguised as a trainer to encourage her son Peisidoros who was taking part in the games. In her enthusiasm for his victory, she ran to embrace her son in wild enjoyment. As she was jumping over the trainers' enclosure wall, however, her chiton fell down and revealed her femininity. The Hellanodikai, however, forgave her her deceit and spared her life out of respect to her family, the Diagorides, who had distinguished three generations of Olympic winners: her father Diagoras, her brothers Eukleus and Kallianaktas and her son Peisidorus. This incident probably gave rise, in 396 BC, to the passing of a law which compelled the trainers to attend the stadium naked, like the athletes.

It is also said that in 448 BC fate had in store for Kallipateira's father, Diagoras, a most glorious death. The old man, who had come to Olympia to watch the games, had the good fortune of seeing both of his sons Olympic winners on the same day. His sons ran close to him, lifted him up in their arms and after crowning him with their crowns, were carrying him among the crowd which was applauding and throwing flowers. Just then a Spartan shouted to the proud father "Κάτθανε Διαγόρα (γιατί δεν θα λάβεις μεγαλύτερη τιμή)", "Now die Diagoras (because you won't receive a bigger honour). You won't ascend to Olympus". Whereupon the old man breathed his last in the arms of his Olympic-winning sons.

Famous Olympic Winners of Antiquity

The wrestler, Milon from Croton, took part in seven Olympiads of which he won six: the 60th (540 BC), in which he probably took part as a child as children were accepted up to the age of 18, the 62nd (532 BC), 63rd (528 BC), 64th (524 BC), 65th (520 BC) and the 66th (516 BC), he lost in the 67th (512 BC), but had managed to maintain his winning streak for a quarter of a century. The Spartan wrestler, Hipposthenes, won five times: in the 39th (624 BC), 40th (620 BC), 41st (616 BC), 42nd (612 BC) and the 43rd (608 BC) Olympiads. The record for victories in the pentathlon was held by the Elean, Gorgos, who won four times at Olympia. He also won once in both the diaulos and the hoplito-dromos. Chonis of Laconia was seven times champion: four times in the stadion and three in the diaulos, in four consecutive Olympiads from 668 BC to 656 BC. The record, however, is held by Leonidas from Rhodes who was twelve times Olympic champion in four consecutive Olympiads, three times in each (stadion, diaulos and hopli-todromos,) from 164 BC to 152 BC. Arrachion the Arcadian was three times Olympic winner in the pankration. He won in the 52nd (572 BC) and 53rd (568 BC) Olympiads and in the 54th Olympiad (564 BC) his rival, during a tactical manoeuvre, squeezed his hands around the neck of Arrachion until he suffocated. Arrachion somehow managed to break his opponent's finger who fainted but, unfortunately, Arrachion died of suffocation at the same time. The Hellanodikai, however, still declared him the winner.

THE RITUAL AND ADMINISTRATION
OF THE GAMES

On the first day of the games, a wild boar was sacrificed to Zeus by the athletes who afterwards swore and oath that they had exercised well during the last 10 months.

From the 77th Olympiad (472 BC), the games lasted for five days and the programme was laid out as follows:

On the first day, the opening ceremony of the games was carried out with great festivity in the morning with a celebration in the Bouleutirion. Here the athletes registered and, infront of the statue of *Zeus Horkios*, after the sacrifice of a wild boar, they, their trainers as well as the fathers and brothers of the young athletes, all took a vow. The athletes vowed that they had completed their ten-month training and that they would compete fairly and without violating the rules. Finally, the Hellanodiaki took a vow to be honest and fair in their judgements and that the would not reveal anything they would learn during the carrying out of their duties. Afterwards, the Hellanodikai and the athletes went to the stadium, passing the Krypte where the priestess of *Demeter Chamyne* welcomed them.

The second day included the horse races and the chariot races in the Hippodrome, whilst in the afternoon the events for the pentathlon took place. The day finished with the mortuary ritual in honour of Pelops, which were a reminder of the original character of the games.

The third day was the most important one of the Games. It overlapped with the next day after the full moon and included glorious rites all devoted to the worship of Zeus. In the morning, an offering of one hundred oxen was given to the god by the Eleans. The large festive procession consisting of the priests, the athletes, the Hellanodikai, the notables of Elis and the Theoroi of all the Greek cities, together with the crowd, started from the Prytaneion, continued along the Processional Way and headed, via the South Gate, to the sacred Altis and the Great Altar of Zeus. Here the large sacrifice of a hundred oxen was made in honour of Zeus. In the afternoon of the same day, the foot races —the stadion, diaulos and dolichos— were held.

On the fourth day the heavy events —the wrestling, boxing, the pankration and the race in armour— were held.

On the fifth and last day of the games, the festive awarding of the prizes to the winners was carried out on the pronaos of the Temple of Zeus, in front of the statue of the god. The crowns were placed on a gold and ivory table made by Colotes, the student of Pheidias, and kept in the Heraion. With these the Hellanodikai crowned the Olympic winners amongst

Representation on a red-figured kylix of the 5th century BC showing two athletes holding strigils ready to clean their bodies of the oil and sand which covered them during the exercises.
(Vatican Museum)

the applause of the crowd who were throwing flowers and leaves. After the awarding of the prizes, a feast was held in the Prytaneion, in honour of the winners, which the representatives the Greek cities and the official guests of the sanctuary also attended. During the night, the hymns and songs of the friends and relatives of the winners echoed through the peaceful valley of Olympia and the victory celebrations would last until the next morning.

THE HERAIA

Besides the Olympic Games for men, every four years in Olympia were also held, from very early times, the Heraia, which were foot races for women in honour of Hera. As it appears, these female games were even more ancient than the Olympic games. As mentioned above, according to the alternate periods of 49 and 50 months between each, the Olympic games were held either in the month of Apollonios (August/September), or the month of Parthenios (September/October). This alternation was probably a convenience for the sake of the Heraia, in order that the two games would not be held at the same time. The Heraia were games of pre-Dorian origin which, according to the myth, were organized for the first time by Hippodamia in her desire to honour Hera and express her gratitude for her marriage to Pelops. In the historical years, the organization of the games was carried out by sixteen women from prominent Elean families who also acted as the judges. Every four years, sixteen female Eleans wove the peplos of the goddess; placed it, with honours, on the statue of Hera in her temple during the holding of the Heraia, and organized a foot race for virgins. The virgins were divided, according to their ages, into three categories and had to run the race which covered a distance equal to 5/6th of the stadium.

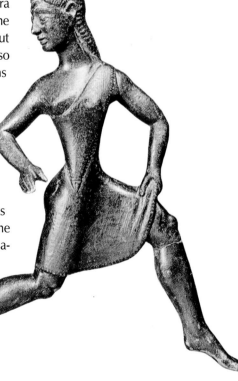

Bronze statuette of a female athlete from Sparta in a race from antiquity. (British Museum, London)

The winner was crowned with an olive branch and gained strength from Hera after eating the meat she was given from the cow which was sacrificed to the goddess. She also had the right to erect her image in the Heraion. Pausanias, who preserved the relevant myth, also presents us with a description of the kore-athlete who participates in the Heraia: she has her long loose hair on her shoulders and wears a short chiton, reaching down to just above the knee, which reveals her right shoulder as far as the breast.

THE OLYMPIC EVENTS

The Olympic events were separated into those in which the athletes competed naked, which were held in the stadium, and the horse races, held in the hippodrome.

The programme of Olympic events included the following:

a) **The stadion**: a foot race the length of the stadium. The athletes stopped at the end of the stadium without returning to the starting line.

b) **The diaulos**: a foot race the length of two stadia, where the athletes finished at the starting line of the stadium.

c) **The dolichos** or **long distance race**: a foot race which probably had a length of twenty four stadia. This event was probably connected to the spondophoroi of the Sacred Truce who were running across the whole country to announce the Truce. A notable dolichos runner and Olympic winner was Ageus who, on the same day of his victory, ran from Olympia to his homeland of Argos to announce his victory.

d) **The hoplitodromos** or **race in armour**: a foot race the length of two stadia where the runners were dressed in full armour.

e) **The pentathlon**: an athletic event made up of five separate events —a stadion, the discus, the javelin, jumping and wrestling. The winner was the athlete who came first in three of the five events. The pentathlon, according to Aristotle, is the "best event of the Greeks" because it is the embodiment of the ideal type of athlete; powerful, fast and flexible.

f) **Boxing**: one of the most popular events. The training of the athletes was carried out in the Palaestra by the men who had pronounced muscular physiques. The rules of this event were defined by Onomastos of Smyrna who was an Olympic winner in 688 BC. The family of Diagoras of Rhodes were eminent boxers of the 5th century BC, claiming Olympic victories by the father, three sons and two grandsons.

g) **The pankration**: an event which combined boxing and wrestling. It is a violent event that placed the physical well-being, and many times the life, of the athletes in danger. One famous pankratist was the Thessalian, Polydamas.

The horse races, which were held in the hippo-drome, were enriched through the centuries with the following events:

a) According to myth, in the first chariot race Pelops, the king of Pisa, beat Oenomaus and Heracles beat Cycnus, the son of Ares, in a horse race, thereby establishing these two events.

b) In 680 BC, the *tethrippon* chariot race (with four horses) was added.

c) In 648 BC, the *Teleion Keliton*, or Perfect Horses, races were added.

d) In 500 BC, the apene races with two mules pulling the chariot, were added.

e) In 496 BC, the *calpe* or *anabates* (races for mares) were added.

f) in 408 BC, *synoris* horse races, a chariot race with two horses pulling the chariot, were added.

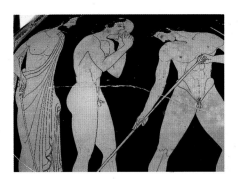

g) In 384 BC, chariot races with four colts were added.

h) In 268 BC, synoris races with colts were added, and

i) In 256 BC, the horse races with colts were added.

Guardian of the horse races was *Poseidon Hippius*. The winner in these events was proclaimed, not the charioteer, but the owner of the chariot or horse and they were crowned with the olive wreath, whilst the victorious charioteer or rider was crowned with a woolen band. In Olympia, in exceptional circumstances, women were allowed to indirectly participate in the horse races. The first female Olympic winner was Kyniska, daughter of Archidamus, king of Sparta, who won in the chariot races of 396 and 392 BC.

Also, from 396 BC, contests for trumpeters and heralds were included in the programme of the games. According to Pausanias, they were carried out on an altar used as a podium which was in front of the northern part of the Echo Colonnade. Here the contesting trumpeters and heralds stood and the winners offered their services during the games, by trumpeting various commands or announcing the names of the winners. An eminent Olympic winning trumpeter was Herodoros of Megara, who won continuously in ten Olympiads from 328 to 292 BC.

THE OLYMPIC TITLE

The title of Olympic winner gave to an athlete fame, both during his lifetime and posthumously, throughout the entire Greek world. Any differences, political or regional, were overcome and, in the person of the Olympic winner, the immortal Greek ideal was praised. His particular home city participated in his victory and, whilst enjoying the great honour he brought, it also returned it. His proud fellow citizens knocked down a part of the city walls through which the victor, who praised his homeland across Greece, made his entry. The Olympic winner received wide responsibilities in the cultural events of the city and also in religious duties. In Sparta, he was given the honour of fighting on the side of the king. The 'deification' of the winner was completed with the composition of a victory ode written especially for him by a poet, and the building of a statue of the athlete which he offered at a panhellenic sanctuary. As mentioned by Pliny, the statue did not show personal characteristics of the athlete but the ideal of the 'good and honest' man. It became a portrait only in cases of very special success such as would be the case with continuous Olympic victory. On the base were inscribed the full names of the athlete, his homeland, his trainer and also the event he had won. This immortal symbol of victory was offered by the Olympic winner to Zeus, who had bestowed on him his great honour.

An Olympic winner and his trainer are shown crowned with wild olive and proud of their success in attaining this highest honour.

POLITICAL AND CULTURAL CONTRIBUTION OF THE GAMES

The contribution of the Olympic games to the political course of Hellenism is incalculable. At Olympia, a very strong feeling of national awareness developed. The Sacred Truce gave unique opportunities for honest rivalry and a healthy competition which reflected the ideals of the Greek culture in the best possible way. There exists a long list of notables of the, by then, known world who were watching the games: rhetoricians, sophists, philosophers, poets, politicians and historians. To these games are also indebted for their inspiration, the worthy representatives of ancient athletic poetry: Pindar, Simonides and Bacchylides.

Finally, the Archaic and Classical sculpture depicted, in the finest way, the athletic vigour and ideal beauty. The best sculptors of all time studied the strong harmonious physique and showed in their works the 'good and honest' young man;

HELLENISTIC AND ROMAN PERIODS: THE INEVITABLE DECLINE

During the Hellenistic and Roman periods, the appearance of the professionalization of the sports becomes more obvious. At the small regional games, as well as at Olympia, the first cases appear of such dealings as the bribery of the competitors, the buying and selling of victory with the bribery of immoral athletes who agreed to compete as representatives for other cities, unfair competition and the breaking of sacred vows. The decline was substantially assisted by the split of the ancient unity of religion and sport, the social honours and financial benefits the Olympic winners received, along with the opinions of the philosophers of those times who criticized every form of physical exercise. Later, the Romans brought with them an approach to sports which had very little to do with the Greek athletic ideal. Characteristic of this was the barbarian behaviour of Sulla who plundered Olympia and in 80 BC transported the Olympic games to Rome and obliged the athletes to contest for the amusement of the Romans. A century later, the institution suffered its largest blow from the humiliating behaviour of Nero. The philhellenic emperors, Hadrian and Antoninus, wanted to strengthen the prestige of the games and to support the athletic ideal in Greece, but whatever they achieved was destroyed by their heirs. The place where once the Greeks confirmed, with much celebration, their open conviction, ended up as a gathering of tribes with no cultural cohesion. In AD 393, the panhellenic games in Greece were officially abolished by a decree from emperor Theodorius I of Byzantium.

During the years of the emperor Claudius (AD 51 - 54), the Antiochians bought the right to organize the Olympic Games from the Eleans. These games were held every year following the model of the old ones: the athletes contested, as in Olympia, for a simple olive-crown. These games were continued after AD 393 up to AD 520 when the emperor Justinian banned them. In AD 529 the closing of Plato's Academy and of the rest of the philosophical schools, basically meant the inevitable end of the ancient Greek education. The Olympic Games from their foundation in 776 BC up to AD 393, lasted 1,168 years during which time 293 Olympiads were held.

Bronze bust of an athlete of the 5th century BC. The statue of an Olympic winner did not usually show personal characteristics, only those of the 'good and honest' youth, and it was always offered by the athlete to Zeus with whose help the athlete achieved his great vitory.

Copy of the famous Discobulus by Myron. The original is dated to around 450 BC. (Rome, Terme) 115

Chapter

6

THE MODERN OLYMPIC GAMES

- THE IOC
- THE LIGHTING OF THE OLYMPIC FLAME
- THE INTERNATIONAL OLYMPIC ACADEMY (IOA)
- THE MUSEUM OF THE OLYMPIC GAMES
- THE PIERRE DE COUBERTIN MONUMENT
- THE MODERN OLYMPIADS
(Short reference to the Olympic Games
from 1896 until today)

"*The irreplaceable value of the Olympic Games
consists in that they are peculiar celebrations during
which people of all religions, all tribes, all nations
and all ranks can be unified with the others
and during which it is revealed to them the deep
sense of community above every kind
of difference and border.
It is necessary and advantageous to regard
and cultivate the Olympic Games as a great celebration
of the whole of mankind, because in this way
it promotes mankind.*"

Pierre de Coubertin

Evangelos and Konstantinos Zappas

Evangelos Zappas was born in 1800 in Lampovo, a village of the Tepelenio in Epirus. He did not receive any higher education because when he was thirteen years old he was recruited by Ali Pasha. After wandering around in the west, he went to Bucharest in 1831 where the notables of Vlachia accepted him warmly because of his character and also the practical knowledge of surgery he had gained from his service in the army. His cousin, Konstatinos Zappas, was born in 1812. When he grew up, he also went to Vlachia where, together with Evangelos, he was involved in the cultivation of large fields which they purchased and amassed a great fortune. Evangelos Zappas died on the 19th of June 1865 and in his will he declared that that Building of the Olympians should be built in Athens according to the plans he had sent to Alexandros Rangavis, in order that the Olympiads he had sponsored in the past could take place there. He left all his fortune to his cousin, Konstantinos, under the condition that he manage it as he thought best for as long as he should live, but after his death he was to leave it to the Greek nation. Konstantinos not only managed the fortune extremely well, he also made it larger and at the same time carried out many beneficial acts. He founded the Zappian Girls Schools in Constaninople and Adrianoupolis, as well as in Lampovo, his homeland, and the Zappio Megaro in Athens, the Building of the Olympians Evangelos had designed and which Konstantinos visited during its opening ceremony in 1884 during the 4th Olympiad. Konstantinos died in the town of Mandon, France, on the 21st of January 1892. In his will, he left his and Evangelos' fortune to the Greek nation.

The first attempts to re-establish the Olympic Games, the crowning athletic event in the history of mankind, were made in the middle of the 19th century. The municipality of Letrinoi (today the town of Pyrgos, west of Olympia) was the first in 1838, 58 years before the first modern Olympiad. Ioannis Chryssafis mentions this initiative in his historical book 'ΟΙ ΣΥΓΧΡΟΝΟΙ ΟΛΥΜΠΙΑΚΟΙ ΑΓΩΝΕΣ', 'The Modern Olympic Games', along with the decision of the municipality of Letrinoi to hold the Olympic games in Pyrgos of Elis every four years. He ends as follows "... I did not manage to find any more additional information which would help me to conclude if these games were held...". In 1850, Minas Minoidis, another Greek living in Paris, suggested the re-establishment of the games, publishing the 'Γυμνα-στικόν', 'Gymnastikon' of Philostratos, a book which he found on Mount Athos. These praiseworthy initiatives continued with the Zappian Olympiads financed by the foundation of the national benefactor Evangelos Zappas.

With a special decree of the 19th of August 1858, a decision was made to hold in Athens "General contests carried out every four years under the name OLYMPIA, with the intention of showing to everyone the products of Greek power and especially of industry, agriculture and livestock...". This decree included also "with the expenses of the state, gymnastic events in the stadium, suitably arranged...". They also included intellectual contests with a written and musical work awarded as the prize. These first Olympic Games, even though they were classed as a fiasco owing to the trade exhibition they included, were held on the 15th of November 1859.

Organizations such as these, with a naturally limited character on a national level were, however, paving the way for the events at the end of the 19th century.

The re-establishment of the great institution is inseparably connected to the Frenchman, Baron Pierre de Coubertin. Born in Paris in 1863, he went to the military school of Saint-Cyr and almost from the start showed an interest in sociology and pedagogics. The French peer studied the history of ancient Greece with great devotion and dreamt of an educational system which was not based on the donnish education of his time but on a different educational base which aimed for the development of people with courage and wisdom. During his studies of the history of ancient Greece, he was impressed by the magnificence and sensation which the Olympic games had in antiquity.

Coubertin thus proposed the organization and holding of the Olympic games, defining also the idealogical content of the institution: the necessary international character of the games with the inclusion of the majority of the sports which would aim to develop friendship and co-operation among the nations, the stabilization of worldwide peace and the abolition of racial discrimination and, finally, the necessary foundation of an international committee who would be the trustees of 'Olympism'. His first address was made in the amphitheatre of the Sorbonne in 1892. In 1894, during the international congress for the study and spread of the principles of athletics which were held in Paris, his proposal for the re-establishment of the Olympic games was accepted and the International Olympic Committee was founded, with Dimitris Vikelas as president and Pierre de Coubertin as secretary general. In accordance with Coubertin's proposal, the Olympic games would be held every four years but each time in a different country. At this congress, Greece was represented by Dimitris Vikelas who had been appointed representative of the Panhellenic Gymnastic Association. Besides Greece and France, representatives attended from England, the Netherlands, Italy, Australia, America, Sweden, Spain, Russia, Belgium, Hungary and Bohmeia. Pierre de Coubertin wanted to give the honour to Greece which was hers from antiquity and so he suggested, and it was accepted, that the first modern Olympic games should be held in Athens. With regard to Coubertin's decision, in the first issue of the Bulletin of the International Olympic Committee appeared the following: "... The fruitful idea for the re-establishment of these games is an idea basically Greek and it was an act of justice to hold the first ones on the ground where they were born."

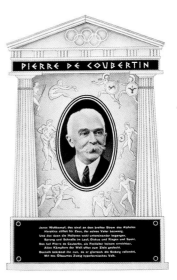

Pierre de Coubertin.

THE IOC

The International Olympic Committee, as resulted from the 1894 Paris congress, is an organization of international prestige and radiance which, according to Coubertin comprises "the laying of the foundations of the Olympic idea". It has general control of the Olympic games which are assigned every time to one city and not to a country, following a relevant application by that city. During the organization of the games, the IOC co-operates with the National Olympic Committee of every country in the city in which the games will be held. The IOC consists of 75 members who, in accordance with the statutes of the association, are lifetime members and can only resign voluntarily. Their members are ambassadors of the Olympic Movement throughout the whole world but are not representatives of their respective countries and thus remain free from governmental interventions or other interests.

Head of the IOC is its president who undertakes its management. The first president of the IOC was D. Vikelas. After the first modern Olympic games in Athens, the presidency was assumed by Pierre de Coubertin who organized the Olympic Games of 1900 in Paris. He remained in this position until 1924. Since 1915, the headquarters of the Committee have been in Lausanne, Switzerland.

THE LIGHTING OF THE OLYMPIC FLAME

Since Olympiad XI, in Berlin in 1936, the enactment of a glorious ceremony has been established which symbolizes the historical continuance of the Games and their strong bonds with ancient Olympia. The lighting of the Olympic Flame is carried out on the altar in front of the Temple of Hera. A group of girls, dressed in ancient-style garments, gather around the altar whilst their leader, who carries out the duties of the *prothereia*, or vestal priestess, lights a torch from the rays of the sun using a metallic reflector. The prothereia then gives the sacred flame, which has already been placed in a special vessel containing an inflammable material, to a runner who carries it first to the memorial of Pierre de Coubertin, where he lights the altar in honour of the ardent supporter and reviver of the Olympic Spirit. The flame is then carried by thousands of athletes, first to Athens and then to the city which has

THE INTERNATIONAL OLYMPIC ACADEMY (IOA)

In 1949, during a session of the IOC in Rome, in line with a proposal by Ioannis Ketseas, the decision was taken to found the International Olympic Academy which was put into practice twelve years later in 1961. Today, close to the ancient stadium, in an area of 900 acres are the superb installations of the Academy. Every year, thousands of athletes and people involved in sports from all over the world are accommodated here, where they exchange views and hold congresses in the context of the Olympic Spirit.

The International Olympic Academy.

THE MUSEUM OF THE OLYMPIC GAMES

In addition, there is in Olympia, under the care of the Greek Committee of the Olympic Games, the Museum of the Modern Olympic Games, which was set up after a proposal by G. Papastefanou. In the museum are exhibitions of rare objects connected to the modern Olympiads, such as Olympic coins, medals of Olympic winners, torches which were used to transport the Olympic flame as well as rich photographic material. Of great interest is the presentation of each modern Olympiad held which is accompanied by relevant posters, pictures, lists of Olympic winners, various documents, medals and other items. The 'prize' of the Museum, however, is the famous and unique stamp collection of the founder of the Museum, G. Papastefanou. This collection follows the subject of the Modern Olympic Games of the last 100 years and is accompanied by related informative microfilms.

The monument to the French baron and great visionary, Pierre de Coubertin.

THE PIERRE DE COUBERTIN MONUMENT

As a minimal tribute in memory of the character of the man who dreamt of, and succeeded in bringing about, the revival of this great athletic institution, Greece erected a simple monument in the area known as the 'Coubertin Grove'. In this monument, the embalmed heart of the great Hellenist is kept, which was brought to Greece by his wife a year after his death in 1938.

THE OLYM

From 1896 to 2004

Through the years, the Olympic Games have managed to win their rightful place in history. They are still the highest ambition of athletes all over the world. Though the olive branch has been replaced by a gold medal and the exalting songs of the ancient world by tempting prizes for the winners of the modern Games, the glory that comes from an Olympic victory remains exactly the same.

The modern history of the Olympic Games begins in 1896, and from then to now it has lasted through both difficulties and moments of sheer magnificence. The only Olympiads not to have been held were those scheduled for 1916, 1940 and 1949 due to the outbreak of the two World Wars. The honour of hosting the Games has always been great, but the task extremely difficult. The undertaking of the countries who organize the Games offers, each time, the opportunity for a different country to play host and thus promises a different dimension to the games. There have been many times when there were notable failures, but the creation of the Winter Olympics, along with the Paralympics for disabled athletes, brought the institution of the Games back to its initial form, giving it the breath of equality, social justice and human sensitivity. In addition, long before the introduction of these Games, the participation of female athletes had been established which came as a victory parallel to the, by then, still fresh appearance of the feminine movement.

Slowly, the concept of marketing and advertising came to complete and complement the organization of the games. But did not they not come also from the ancient Olympic Games? It is said that the winners of ancient Greece, as well as the olive wreath, also received an amount oil, the origin of which was announced loudly to the people of the area so that the victory of the athlete remained in the minds of the spectators along with the quality of the oil he was awarded.

Through glorious moments and critical comments the Olympic Games have never ceased to represent only one thing: Man. His life. His story.

THE MODERN OLYMPIC GAMES

I	1896	Athens	6th April - 15th April
II	1900	Paris	14th May - 28th October
III	1904	St. Louis	1st July - 23rd November
IV	1908	London	27th April - 31st October
V	1912	Stockholm	5th May - 22nd July
VI	1916	Berlin	

(The Games did not take Place due to the outbreak of the First World War)

VII	1920	Antwerp	7th July - 12th September
VIII	1924	Paris	4th May - 27th July
IX	1928	Amsterdam	17th May - 12th August
X	1932	Los Angeles	30th July - 14th August
XI	1936	Berlin	1st August - 16th August
XII	1940	Tokyo	

(The Games did not take place due to the war between Japan and China. Permission to organize the games was given to Finland but the Games still did not take place due to the outbreak of the Second World War)

XIII	1944	London	

(These Games were also not held due to the Second World War)

XIV	1948	London	29th July - 14th August
XV	1952	Helsinki	19th July - 3rd August
XVI	1956	Melbourne	22nd November - 8th December
XVII	1960	Rome	25th August - 11th September
XVIII	1964	Tokyo	10th October - 24th October
XIX	1968	Mexico	12th October - 27th October
XX	1972	Munich	26th August - 11th September
XXI	1976	Montreal	17th July - 1st August
XXII	1980	Moscow	19th July - 3rd August
XXIII	1984	Los Angeles	28th July - 12th August
XXIV	1988	Seoul	17th September - 2nd October
XXV	1992	Barcelona	25th July - 8th August
XXVI	1996	Atlanta	19th July - 4th August
XXVII	2000	Sydney	15th September - 1st October
XXVIII	2004	Athens	13th August - 29th August
XXIX	2008	Beijing	

Glossary

Akroterion: *decorative element at the apex and both ends of a pediment.*

Antefix: *the covers at the edges of a roof on all four sides of a building. The cover tiles are the second layer which cover the joints of the first layer of tiles on the roof. They end in decorative relief representations of anthemions, female heads, Silenoi etc.*

Aphrodite of Cnidus: *a work by Praxiteles of the 4th century BC which has not survived. Extremely revealing for its accurate sculpture and because the artist represented the goddess completely naked.*

Caduceus: *the symbol of Hermes, the messenger god. A narrow stick of laurel around which are entwined two snakes and on top of which it had wings.*

Cella: *the interior chamber of a temple between the side walls; the sanctuary. It is the main part of the temple where the worshipped statue was erected.*

Centaurs: *wild creatures, half man half horse. They lived in the Mountains of Pelion and Orsa of Thessaly.*

'Corinthian'-style Helmet: *The most common helmet type. Made out of a single sheet of metal which covered almost the whole face, except the eyes and mouth, and the nape of the neck.*

Daedalic Goddesses: *works which, by their style, belong to the so-called 'Daedalic' art which chronologically covers the greatest part of the 7th century BC. According to RJH Jenkins,* its beginnings are around 680 BC, *(whilst G. Rizza maintains that the Daedalic phase of Greek art begins at the turn of the 7th century). The basic characteristic of Daedalic art is the severe organization of the figures based on the horizontal and vertical axes which govern the natural forms.*

Diazoma: *horizontal level separating the seats in a theatre and from where the spectators go to their seats.*

Dresden Zeus: *The original work is dated to around 450 to 440 BC. It is said to be the work of Pheidias. The most important copy of it is on display in Dresden.*

Embankment: *sloping ground, where the spectators were sitting or standing, created usually by banking or smoothing of the ground that surrounded the stadium. In the beginning this was done on only two sides and later on three and finally on all four.*

Entablature: *the upper part of an order consisting of the architrave, frieze and cornice.*

Episphyrion: *ribbon used to attach the greave; the protective cover for the ankle and part of the defensive arms of the hoplite soldiers.*

Griffins: *mythical animals with the body of a lion and the head of an eagle. Mainly known in nearby Anatolia from where they passed into the Minoan, and from there to ancient Greek, mythology and art.*

"Hermes Richelieu": *The original work of the 4th century BC has not survived. The most important copy is exhibited in the Louvre.*

Hyperoon: *area above the side nave of a temple. In the Hellenistic basilica the hyperoon was above the side nave and the narthex, from where the women watched the service, giving this area the name gynaikonite or women's nave.*

'Illyrian'-style Helmet: *this helmet is known by this name because it was first found in the northern Balkans. It is an entirely Greek helmet which first appeared in the Peloponnese at the beginning of the 7th century BC and very much later in Illyria and other regions. The helmets of this style are light, had protective guards only for the cheeks and were often decorated with relief representations of animals.*

Kamilos the Alexandrian: *an important wrestler from Alexandria.*

Lapiths: *a tribe of Thessaly. Their king, Pirithous, was a friend of Theseus.*

Lepreos: *an ancient town and acropolis in Southern Triphylia (western Peloponnese). It is believed to have been founded by Lepreus, son of Pyrgeas. 40 Stadia from the sea and 100 stadia from Samiko. It has been identified by Curtius with the hills north of the present-day village of Lepreos.*

Metope: *a slab of stone, smooth and decorated with reliefs which, on the Doric frieze, alternates with triglyphs.*

Nave: *the areas into which the interior of a building is separated by the columns.*

Obeloi: *functional utensils of the clergy, made of metal, in the shape of a stick.*

Obsidian: *Volcanic rock formed by a particular type of lave, rich in silicon dioxide. It was widely used in all Greek regions during Stone Age and Bronze Age for the making of tools, spear heads, blades etc.*

Palladium: *According to the myth, when the goddess Athena was still a young girl, she was brought up in the house of the god Triton whose daughter, Pallas, was as equally talented as Athena in the art of war. During a fight between the two girls, Athena killed Pallas by accident in front of Zeus. The goddess, suffering the loss of her friend, used her considerable technical ability to build the famous Palladium (a wooden statue) in the likeness of her friend. She put it under her aegis and described its divine honours. In art it is normally noted as a statuette depicting the goddess Athena.*

Sima: *this was usually only on the sides of the temple and had two main functions: it was there to hold the rain water and it served as a decorative crowning to the building. In many temples it was also there to catch the run-off from the roof. For this purpose, it had equally spaced pipes or lion-head water spouts. On temples of the 4th century BC, the sima had relief decorations of plants.*

Strigils: *special rectangular tools of bronze or iron, used by the athletes for cleaning their bodies of the oil and sand they threw on themselves during their exercises.*

Telchines: *according to the myth, they were born of the sea and were the first ones to inhabit Rhodes. They are particularly known as metallurgists and inventive craftsmen. It is said that they were the first ones to finely work iron and bronze and made many wonderful works such as Cronus' sickle and Poseidon's trident.*

The Twelve Labours of Heracles: *represented in the Temple of Olympia for the first time are twelve traditional labours of Heracles. According to M. Andronikos, this was the first time in the history of Greek art that they were pictorialized.*

Triglyph: *a decorative element of the Doric frieze which alternates with the metopes and is formed by three grooves, or glyphs.*

Bibliography

1. N. ALEXOPOULOU, *Οι αγώνες διαμέσου των αιώνων* (1930)
2. A. et N. GIALOURI, *ΟΛΥΜΠΙΑ, ΟΔΗΓΟΣ ΤΟΥ ΜΟΥΣΕΙΟΥ ΚΑΙ ΤΟΥ ΙΕΡΟΥ*, Athens 1993
3. ANTOINETTE KALLEGIA, *ΟΛΥΜΠΙΑ*, Athens 1993
4. A. KARAKATSANI - TH. STATHAKOPOULOU, *ΑΧΑΪΑ- ΗΛΕΙΑ*, Εθνική Τράπεζα της Ελλάδος, Athens 1973
5. E. KARPIDINI - DIMITRIADI, *ΠΕΛΟΠΟΝΝΗΣΟΣ*, Athens 1996
6. I. KONTIS, *Το ιερόν της Ολυμπίας κατά τον Δ' αιώνα π. Χ.*, Athens 1958
7. C. BECK, *Ολυμπιακοί Αγώνες 1896*, Athens 1906
8. XENOPHON, *ΕΛΛΗΝΙΚΑ*
9. N. PAPACHATZIS, *Παυσανίου Ελλάδος Περιήγησις Μεσσηνικά - Ελληνικά* (1979)
10. N. PETROPOULOU, *Οδηγός Αρχαίας Ολυμπίας*, Athens 1936
11. STRAVON, *ΓΕΩΓΡΑΦΙΚΑ*
12. Γ. TARASOULEAS, *Ολυμπιάδες στην Αθήνα* (1978)

13. B. ASMOLE-N. YALOURIS, *Olympia. The Sculptures of the Temple of Zeus*, London 1967
14. F. M. CORNFORD, *The Origin Of the Olympic Games* (1912)
15. W. DORPFELD, *Alt -Olympia* (1935)
16. E.N. GARDINER, *Olympia; Its history and Remains*, Oxford 1925
17. E.N.GARDINER, *Athletics in the Ancient World*, Oxford 1930
18. W.W. HYDE, *Olympic Victor Monuments and Greek Athletic Art* (1921)
19. J. SWANDLING, *The Ancient Olympic Games*, London 1980
20. N. YALOURIS, *Olympia* (The Princeton Encyclopedia of Classial Sites, Princeton 1976)

21. EKDOTIKI ATHINON, *ΙΣΤΟΡΙΑ ΤΟΥ ΕΛΛΗΝΙΚΟΥ ΕΘΝΟΥΣ*
22. EKDOTIKI ATHINON, *Η ιστορία των Ολυμπιακών Αγώνων*, Athens 1982

23. *Πρακτικά της Διεθνούς Ολυμπιακής Ακαδημίας*
24. *Λεύκωμα Β' Διεθνών Ολυμπιακών Αγώνων*, Athens 1907
25. *Λεύκωμα της Ηπείρου*, Athens 1911
26. *Ιστορία της Επιτροπής των Ολυμπιακών Αγώνων*, Athens 1995
27. *Ημερολόγιον της Μεγάλης Ελλάδος*, Athens 1925 - 1926
28. *Les jeunes olympiques dans l' antiquite et de nos jours,* Editions Rhea, Paris 1925

Text: ANNA MAPANTI
Translation: CHRISSI NERANTZI and ADAM FRANK
Artistic Supervision: MICHAEL LACENERE

Colour separations - Layout and Printing: M. TOUBIS S.A.